Start a 6-F

Junk Removaı

Business

A Complete Guide to Setting Up a Profitable Junk Removal Service

By: Michael Mettlach

Snap Enterprise LLC

Start a 6-Figure Junk Removal Business

Printed in the United States of America

First Printing, 2016

Snap Enterprise LLC
14018 Pine Meadow Ln
Tomball, TX 77377

Table of Contents:

Chapter 1: Crash Course in the Junk Removal Biz

Simple business snap shot

At its core the junk removal business is relatively simple. You go to peoples' houses and haul away the trash they tell you to get rid of. They pay you to take it, and you haul it to your local landfill and pay to dump it. I believe the simplicity of this business is what attracts me and so many other people to it, but despite this simplicity, there are many details involved in the daily operations of a junk hauling business that can trip a beginner up or temporarily halt their success. My goal in writing this book is to provide you with a clear path, free from fear of the unknown, to setting up and running a profitable junk removal business.

So how does a day in a junk removal business typically unfold? Hopefully you'll wake up before your alarm goes to the sound of your business phone ringing. On the other end will be a potential customer wondering how your service and pricing works, and how soon you can make it out to haul off their household items and furniture from their recent move. You'll schedule them for later that day if you have time, or maybe for the next day or two depending on your schedule. Then you'll wake up and get ready for work. Your labor helper/driver will then show up and drive you to the local landfill first thing in the morning to dump your previous days' load. After spending 40 minutes in traffic and another 20 at the landfill sitting in line and then dumping, you're ready for your first job of the day. You pay $75 at the landfill because your trash weighed a little over a ton and they charged you by weight.

So you map your first job of the day and then you call the customer (or text) to tell them you're in route and you're about forty minutes away. On a typical decent day you might have 3 different jobs spaced 2 to 3 hours apart. On your way to the first job you might get a few more calls, some will be telemarketers, some will be customers just seeking information on pricing but are too cheap, and maybe one in five will be an actual scheduling paying customer. It's a good thing you have a driver to free up your time to answer calls and schedule jobs. Forty minutes later you show up to job number one. It's a garage clean out. You load up a couch, a loveseat, some random boxes of household goods, and some scrap lumber out of the garage. The customer tries to get you to take some paint and oil, but you decline, it's against your policy (and illegal for you to take). All in all it takes you only 15 minutes to load, but you charge $200 plus tax, because it filled half your trailer, and you charge based on volume, not time. They hand you a check, and then your team is off to the next job.

You map job #2 to then call the customer and tell them you're on the way. But wait, you're running early and the customer can't make it early because they are too far away. Bummer, looks like you have to go waste some time at a gas station near the job and pay your worker to do nothing for half an hour. After you burn 30 minutes you spend another 30 minutes on the way to the next job. You arrive and surprise surprise, they have a big screen TV that they forgot to tell you was upstairs, and their reclining couch is upstairs as well. You and your worker proceed to muscle the heavy couch downstairs avoiding scraping paint on the walls and rubbing the doorway as you exit, and then decide that the big screen rear projection TV is too precariously heavy and awkward to maneuver downstairs and around corners, so you spend another 20 minutes taking it apart upstairs by unscrewing and unbolting a few fasteners, and finally whisk it down the stairs in 3 or 4 pieces, safely and easily. The customer contemplates and then decides to add an old rusty BBQ pit to the load. You charge them $150 plus tax and they pay with a credit card. Even though you still have about an eighth of your trailer still empty, you decide you had better take this load to the landfill, because you know an eighth of a trailer is not sufficient space to accommodate the next job, which is a large construction waste job. You spend another 40 minutes in traffic and then another 20 minutes at the landfill dumping. You end up spending $64 at the dump ($44 per ton minimum, plus $25 pull-off fee, plus taxes). Looks like you made $286 ($350-$64) on this load before overhead and various expenses, not bad.

Finally you head to your 3rd and last job of the day. You let the customer know you're on the way and on your 30 minute trek to the gig you return 2 phone calls that you missed while you were at the landfill. One of them pans out and you schedule another garage clean out for the next day. After thirty minutes you arrive at job number 3. You knock on the door and the customer proceeds to escort you to a monstrous pile of boards, sheet rock, kitchen cabinets, and some branches in the back yard, about 40 feet away from where you could park your trailer. You inform the customer that you do charge a little extra for construction waste because of the weight involved and difficulty in loading, and after a little hesitation, they agree that this is no problem and tell you to get started. It's a good thing that you brought a garden cart and a wheel barrow, otherwise this construction waste job would take FOREVER. Two hours and a lot of sweat later, you and your helper finally finish loading the remodeling waste heap. It is a completely full trailer, and then some. You get paid a whopping $450 plus tax, and you don't feel bad charging it because a roll-off container would cost the customer almost as much, but it wouldn't load itself. Unfortunately the landfill is closing before you have time to get there, especially since its rush hour traffic, so you and your helper drive back to your facility. You figure you'll end up spending $115 dollars dumping today's load the next day since a trailer load of construction waste is typically about 2 tons.

Now let's examine what the business made on this realistic hypothetical day:

Revenue = 200 + 150 + 450 = $800

Dump fees = 64 + 115 = $179

Labor (helper)= 8 hrs x 13/hr = $104

Labor (you) = 8 hrs x 13/hr = $104

Marketing expense (10% of revenue average) = 800 x .10 = $80

Vehicle expense = $0.55 per mile x 120 miles = $66

Prorated insurance, facility, phone, other overhead = $40 (estimated)

Business Profit = 800-179-104-104-80-66-40 = $227

So in a typical day, running one crew and one truck, it is not unreasonable for your junk removal business to make around $200 dollars, not including whatever wage you decide to allocate to yourself if you are doing some of your own labor. You might conclude that on this typical day you personally made about $331 ($227 + $104 labor) depending on how you want to look at it. If you can consistently meet a sales goal of $800 a day 250 days a year at a 25% profit margin ($200 a day), your business stands to profit $50,000 for each crew you are running.

Unfortunately, while these calculations are not unrealistic, they are somewhat idealistic and do not reflect all the problems that can and will occur during the daily operation of a junk removal business, nor do they represent some of the pleasant surprises you will encounter that will make your business more profitable. Such is the purpose of the discourse contained in the rest of this book.

Anyway, enough story telling. Let's jump into some more specifics on what a successful junk removal business model looks like. We'll take a broad view at first, and then get into way more specific in later chapters.

Marketing: how do you get customers?

Set up a website first. Then advertise on free websites such as craigslist, facebook groups, and online directory listings such yelp, Angies list, and thumbtack, then graduate to paid advertising such as Google adwords, Bing ads, mini-billboards, and facebook paid advertising. Networking on linked in and facebook is also free. Make sure you ALWAYS answer your phone or get back to customers quickly. Don't EVER stop advertising even if you are busy.

Pricing:

There are two main ways you can charge, an upfront volume based rate or in person onsite quote. I personally charge $25 per cubic yard (volume based) of household and furniture waste and $30 per cubic yard for construction and remodeling waste (not including tile, dirt, and masonry products). Major companies like college hunks haul junk or 1800-got, however, typically do a quote up front when they get to a job, which is loosely based on volume but also takes into account difficulty in loading and weight concerns. There are advantages and disadvantages to both pricing methods.

Scheduling:

You can give customers firm times or time windows. I prefer to give firm times spaced 1-3 hours apart depending on job details and logistic circumstances. My company can schedule 3 or 4 jobs per a crew per a day this way. Major junk removal franchises tend to give people 2 hour time windows. If you can get customers to agree to be at home for longer time windows it will be much to your advantage and less stressful on your logistics. It also creates a higher pressure situation for them to agree to your price since they have invested more time waiting for you and simultaneously exhausted other options. This will also allow your business to cram more jobs in a day and combine more loads.

Tools of the trade:

You need a 2 wheel moving dolly, a 4 wheel garden cart, a trash can, and a sledge hammer at the least. I'd also recommend carrying a wheelbarrow, sawzall, and pry bar, and possibly branch shears, pliers, wire cutters, hex wrenches, screw drivers, and regular wrenches. Some tools are only necessary for demo jobs or for dismantling some furniture or appliances so they can fit out a doorway.

Labor:

I recommend hiring only part time labor, as contractors if you're just starting out, as part-time employees once you gain some traction. Pay between $10-15/hr and consider giving the higher end of the spectrum the longer they stay with you and the harder they work. This is very physically demanding work and not necessarily mentally rewarding. Most major franchises pay $12/hr at the time this book was written. I personally pay close to $14/hr. Don't hire friends and family if you're not willing to fire them.

How big should my truck/trailer be?

The bigger the better, because the more you can haul at a particular job, the more you can charge. You save money on logistics this way too by not having to make return trips and also by gaining the ability to combine loads. Most major franchises have a 15 or 16 cubic yard capacity (1800 GOT JUNK box is roughly 10ft long x 8ft wide x 5ft high). Some go as high as 18 cubic yards (Junk King). Some junk removal business entrepreneurs even use 12ft-20ft box trucks (20-30 yards varies).

I personally use 15-16 cubic yard trailers (roughly 16ft long x 6.5ft wide with 4ft high sides or 400 cubic feet with tandem axles).

You need a significant truck to handle the weights involved in this business. Don't use and F-150 or Chevy 1500 unless you are only planning on handling household goods and furniture (no construction waste). I personally use F350s and Chevy 3500s to haul my trailers. The major franchises typically use an F450 or Isuzu NPR HD outfitted with a 16 cubic yard hydraulic dump box. The trucks typically cost 50,000 and the dump box is an additional $10,000 to install if you go this route.

I wouldn't recommend starting off with anything less than a 12ft trailer with 4ft sides if you can avoid it.

Where do I dump?

You need to do a search for "landfills" or "transfer stations" in your area. They typically don't have very user friendly websites, so YOU WILL HAVE TO pick up the phone and call them to get details on what they charge, what types of waste they do and don't accept, do they accept cash customers and hand unloads, what there hours are, and any other details you are concerned with. Not all dumps are open to the public, so you might hit a few dead ends, it's not a big deal, just pick up a phone and call, they are used to it. Skip to the chapter on landfills, there are too many details to put here.

What kind of insurance do I need?

You will need a commercial auto insurance policy. But not just ordinary commercial auto insurance, it is a more expensive version because you will be transporting waste in large heavy trucks. In Texas it is referred to as "for hire" insurance, and is probably similar in your locality. Talk to your insurance provider. Not all insurance providers offer this type of insurance. If you have trouble, try "Progressive". I know they provide it because that's who I got it through. Expect to pay $160/month or more per a truck.

You should also consider obtaining a $1,000,000 general business liability insurance policy. Don't be intimidated, if you're just starting out small it may cost $60-$80 a month. It covers damage to customers' homes or businesses if you are at fault, and while you won't lose too many residential customers if you don't have it, many business or management companies won't work with you if you don't carry it.

If you are crossing state lines and your truck/trailer is over 10,000 pounds, or if you're truck is over a certain weight limit set by your locality, you may need to be DOT certified, which carries its own set of insurance requirements. For instance, in Texas if your vehicle/trailer combo is over 26,000 pounds you need to be DOT certified. This however does not apply to my business, but you will need to check YOUR local regulations to make sure you are compliant.

There may be other insurances required in your state or city, and you may want to do a little research. In my area however, these are all that is required. We'll discuss more about navigating your local legal concerns in a later chapter.

Do I need licenses/permits? Is it legal?

This one is a little tricky to answer with complete certainty. Ultimately it depends on YOUR local state, county, and city laws. Junk removal isn't regulated in a significant way at the federal level as long as it doesn't involve any form of hazardous waste. State laws may be somewhat generic as well, county laws may be similar to the states, but city laws tend to be a little more specific and pickier. In my city of Houston Texas, I don't need a permit to haul junk. The state of Texas does not regulate my business in a significant way as long I don't put trash in an air tight enclosed container or dispose of it irresponsibly, or haul hazardous waste. If I wanted to do weekly scheduled repeat trash pickup within the city limits of Houston or nearby cities of Tomball or Magnolia however, I would need a permit or license and would have to abide by those localities' insurance and operational requirements to maintain the permit. If I wanted to rent out dumpsters within these city limits, I wouldn't be able to either because some of the cities have a contract with only one waste company that they allow to do this (a legal local monopoly) or because I have to buy a permit first in other instances. However, because junk removal companies are typically providing a service that these other dumpster and weekly solid municipal waste pick companies don't (hauling bulky trash they won't take and/or doing all the loading), the regulations are typically more relaxed and you are not prevented from operating a junk removal service in these jurisdictions. Outside city limits however, these municipal laws and regulations typically don't matter, and you could hypothetically set up a trash route or rent out dumpsters, as long as you're abiding by state and county regulations.

If you are getting stuck on this issue, consider calling some of the state, county, and city authorities. Or consider calling other junk removal companies within your same state, but not the same city so they are not your competitors, and ask them if there are state regulations you should be aware of. I hate giving non-definite answers like this, but I can't analyze 50 different states waste/transport regulations, and all the counties, municipalities, HOAs, special purpose districts contained therein, and regurgitate it to you within this book. As a general rule of thumb, if there are major junk removal franchises like 1-800-GOT-JUNK or College Hunks Haul Junk operating in your area, chances are it's perfectly legal for you to do the same, but you still have to make sure you check up on permits or insurance requirements with the individual cities. I personally do not have to carry any special permits for my operation in the greater Houston area, but I do carry "for hire" commercial vehicle insurance.

Getting Set Up: Basic things you need to do to get started:

1. Form an LLC to operate your business under : $300
2. Get an FEIN number for business purposes
3. Open a bank account under that LLC and get a debit card with it. $12/month
4. Get a sales and use tax permit with your state comptroller if appropriate
5. Open a QuickBooks account and link it to your bank account to track accounting. Get a QuickBooks Gopay account and swiper to take credit cards. $36/month
6. Get a callrail.com account and make at least one business number ($30/month)
7. Buy your website domain and make a website using hostgator or wix or have someone do it for you. $12/month
8. Make a craigslist account, a facebook account, a facebook business account, yelp account, thumbtack account. Start posting ads on craigslist and facebook groups immediately even if you can't do jobs yet; you need to get people in your sales funnel.
9. If you don't have a suitable facility, rent one or rent storage spaces or rent parking lot area.

10. Get your equipment ready; buy at least one 16ft trailer or truck with 16 cubic yard dump box. Preferably more than one trailer so you can combine loads. Buy a dolly, sledge hammer, furniture dolly, garden cart, pry bar, sawzall.
11. Buy commercial vehicle insurance and general business liability insurance $160/month and $70/month
12. Have vinyl lettering installed on your truck/trailers including your website and phone number. $250
13. Hire a part time helper.
14. Find your local landfill and do a test run to familiarize yourself.
15. Start doing jobs
16. Get a Google adwords account and Bing ads account and facebook paid advertising account. Start buying PPC ads. Expect to drop $1,000 a month on advertising and do $10,000+ revenue per month.
17. Buy and advertise on mini-billboards in your area.
18. Spend some more time on SEO
19. Market market market! As long as you have sales the rest can take care of itself.
20. Track mileage, track expenses, improve operations. Pay taxes on time.

Knowing the numbers, lets quantify things!

Revenue target for one crew on one truck should be $400-$800 per a day, depending how aggressive your price structure is. If you run 250 days a year (5 days a week) at $800 a day you get $200,000 revenue.

The profit margin for a junk removal business is 20%-30%. Consequently, if you do $200,000 revenue, your business stands to make $40,000-60,000 pretax profit. Keep in mind when setting your expectations that if you want to make a six figure income, you will likely need to do $500,000 in business a year, and run 3 trucks continuously.

Expect to spend around $1,000 a month on advertising to keep one crew busy. Advertising will probably cost you 10% of your revenue.

Your labor costs will likely be 25%-30% of revenue; depending on how big your jobs are each day, if you send people home early on dead days, and how aggressive your pricing is.

Dump fees may cost you about 20% of your revenue, depending on how creative you are at recycling, reselling, load combining, and other waste diversion techniques.

Fuel and equipment cost will vary greatly depending on if you buy used or buy or lease new trucks, and whether you have trailers. Expect to spend around 5% of revenue on fuel costs and 3%-%12 of revenue on equipment repair/maintenance/purchase.

Your facility may cost you around 8% of revenue.

Average revenue per a job is close to $250, depending on how aggressive your pricing is.

Number of jobs per a crew per a day should be near 3, or 4 on a better day

Number of miles per a day may average 120 miles, depending on service area size and ability to combine loads. For each truck you run, you can expect to put on 30,000-40,000 miles per a year.

Decent 16ft tandem axle trailers should cost near $2,500 new, depending on your location. A 16 cubic yard dump trailer will cost $8,000. Equipping a truck with a hydraulic dump box may cost $7,000-10,000.

Buying a used truck capable of reliably towing 7,000 pound loads will cost $5,000 and up, plus frequent repairs (estimate $0.20 per mile repair cost average). Expect to get 10mpg-16mpg for the kind of trucks you will need to use.

Buying a new truck with appropriate weight capacities will likely cost $50,000 or more, not including a hydraulic dump box. You will probably pay near $1,000 per month for 5 years.

You can expect to spend close to $400 or more per a truck as a start up cost for basic moving equipment like dollies, carts, tools, to start off, unless you find deals on used stuff.

Expect to pay $150 or more per a truck per a month for commercial auto "for hire" insurance. It will be more if you buy a new truck and need full coverage.

General business liability insurance may cost you $60-80 a month starting off.

Cost of customer acquisition may be close to $35 per customer. These are for new customers. Repeat business and referrals will be free, and will account for more of your business as you become established.

The standard beginning territory population size for some of the major junk removal franchises is 250,000 people. Make sure you have at least this many people in your service area, preferably more, and that they are affluent enough to pay for junk removal services.

Your website will cost you around $20 a month for hosting and domain name registration.

Expect to pay $0.50-1.00 per a square ft / month or more for commercial warehouse/office space, depending on your area. Vacant lots can be obtained for cheaper, and storage spaces may be more appropriate for a beginner.

Expect to pay $25-50 per a ton to dump waste by weight or $6-12 per a cubic yard depending on your area and type of waste of dumping by volume prices.

16 cubic yards of household trash and furniture will weigh about 2,000 pounds, and 16 cubic yards of construction/remodeling waste

(boards/sheet rock/cabinets/tub/etc).will weigh 3,500-5,000 pounds. Brick, tile, mortar, roofing, and dirt weigh near 2,000 pounds per a cubic yard and change these estimates dramatically. Concrete, cement, and asphalt can weigh 3,000-4,000 pounds per a cubic yard, so pay special attention to weight concerns when hauling these very dense materials.

Chapter 2: The Art of Dumping

The art of dumping; all about landfills and other methods:

There are two main categories of dump sites you need to consider, landfills and transfer stations, and there is more than one type of each.

1. Landfills
    a. Construction waste only
    b. Municipal Solid Waste and construction waste
    c. Other types that don't affect you as a beginning junk removal business
2. Transfer Stations
    a. Open to public
    b. Private and/or contract only

The main difference between a landfill and a transfer station is that landfills are a several acre plot of land that are the final resting place of the trash where it is put into the ground, and a transfer station is a facility where the trash is temporarily dumped before being transferred (via truck, train, boat, etc) to its final resting place at the landfill. The purpose of the transfer station is to serve as a logistics tool to reduce fuel costs and driving time.

To give you an example, in northwest Houston Texas, much of the weekly trash service waste that gets picked up from the curb by the large compacting dump trucks gets dumped at a "transfer station" named Waste Connections Transfer Station about 20 miles away. This transfer station is located near the center of Houston. After these dump trucks drop their trash, it is bulldozed into a large pile using a bulldozer, and then transferred onto 18-wheelers using an excavator. These large 18-wheelers then drive to the massive landfill in Atascocita, which is about 20 miles east of the Waste Connections Transfer Station, and dump their load in its final resting place. If the city dump trucks that originally collected the trash had to drive to Atascocita every time they loaded up, they would have to drive 30 or 40 miles each way, reach higher speeds, and sit in a lot of traffic. If you do the math, it's more efficient to have a transfer station.

As mentioned above, there are two main types of landfills, construction waste only and municipal solid waste landfills that typically ALSO accept construction waste.

Construction waste only landfills are much more restricted in the types of trash that they accept. They accept trash like boards, sheet rock, roofing, tile, insulation, metal, carpet, sinks, toilets, glass, branches, leaves, and sometimes electronics (depending on which one), but DO NOT accept liquids, paint, food trash, many forms of household trash, putrescible waste (waste that rots like food), chemicals, flammables, oil, solvents, burnt waste, tires, hazardous chemicals, and refrigerants.

Municipal solid waste (MSW) landfills will accept these construction waste materials, but also will accept food trash, some liquids (but not on an industrial scale), putrescible waste, branches, leaves, grass, household chemicals, and just about anything that people throw out on their curb for weekly scheduled trash pickup provided by the city. While the regulations on the types of trash you can dispose of at these landfills are typically more relaxed, it is important to note that they still don't accept what's considered hazardous waste: paint, flammables, solvents, tires, compressed cylinders, recently burned materials, hazardous household chemicals, industrial chemicals and industrial waste, oil, medical waste, and more. (The disposal of hazardous and industrial waste like paint, chemicals, and oil is beyond the scope of this book. Really, you should not even be accepting and transporting these materials without the proper training, permits, licenses, and insurances. A lot of this is regulated at the federal level and additional regulations exist at the state, county, and city levels. Since you're just starting off with this book, leave the hazardous.)

Construction waste landfills tend to be more common because there are less restrictions and permits involved in setting up and operating them, and landfills that accept municipal solid waste tend to be more spread apart. Most landfills will be open to the public and not require some kind of contract to dump there, but they do cost money to dump. There is a common misconception some people have that you can dump trash at landfills for free. In my experience, this is only true sometimes if you are dumping as a resident and not a business. City or county owned landfills will often times allow residents a few free dumps per month or per a year if they can prove they are a resident, because their tax dollars pay for the landfill. Businesses, however, have to pay to dump their waste. Dumping is usually not free if you are operating in a business capacity.

While landfills are often open to the public, transfer stations are often times privately owned and operated, and can be closed to the public. For example, in my hometown of Houston, I can dump at the Waste Connections Transfer Station near central Houston about 20 miles away from my headquarters, but I can't dump at one of the 3 or 4 transfer stations that are actually 10 miles closer to my service area because the companies that own them use them solely for their own trash operations and don't let outsiders in.

So how much does it cost to dump at a landfill or transfers station?

It really depends on which one you go to and what type it is, your location, and if you have some kind of additional contract with them. Ultimately you will have to call each dump individually, and ask about their pricing. Assuming your region is similar to mine, if your landfill is charging based on volume, you can expect to pay $8.50-10.50 per a cubic yard plus a few additional taxes. If your landfill or transfer station is charging by weight, you can expect to pay $30-55 per a ton of trash. If you have a contract worked out with your local dump(s), you may be on the lower end of the spectrum or even lower, but as a beginner, you may not be able to get some kind of contract or lower price, if your dump even has that option. In my experience, most of the landfills are charging based on volume and transfer stations are going to charge by weight. If you have heavy construction waste materials it's not too much of a loss to dump by volume, but if you have less dense waste like furniture and household trash, you stand to save a lot of money by dumping at facilities that charge by weight, not volume. For instance, I can dump a 16 cubic yard trailer overfilled with furniture (1 ton of waste) for $44.67 at my local transfer station because they charge $44 a ton. But, if I took it to one of the local landfills that charges by volume at $10/cubic yard, I would end up paying $160. That's quite a difference.

In general, here are some example values you can expect to pay to dump, assuming you have a 16 cubic yard trailer or dump box:

By volume:

Full Trailer any type of waste = $160

Half Trailer (8 yards) = $80

Eighth Trailer (2 yards) = $45 (because dumps have minimum charges near $45

By weight:

Full Trailer Construction Waste = $100

Half Trailer Construction Waste = $50

Full Trailer Household Trash and Furniture = $50

Half Trailer Household Trash and Furniture = $44 (minimum charge)

Overview of how to dump at the landfill:

Typically any dump you go to will have an office near the front of the facility that you have to check in at before you are allowed to access the rest of the facility. Depending on the facility, they may have a scale out in front at the office to weigh your truck and trailer on, like the scales at a scrap metal yard. If they do, pull up onto the scale before talking to the office person, or if they don't, just pull up next to the office.

If the dump charges by volume, they may have someone come up with a tape measure and measure your trailer or dump box, or they may just have the office person estimate your load volume by looking at it. Once they determine the volume of your load, they will tell you the total price, you will pay them (sometimes cash only, most accept credit card though), and proceed to the rest of the facility to dump your load. Some dumps that make you weigh in at the scales still just charge by volume. Typically if they charge by volume you won't have to weigh out again when you leave.

If the dump charges by weight, you will pull up on the scales to weigh in, and then talk to the office person at the window by the scale. They will probably ask you for a credit card or a cash deposit to hold onto until you weigh out. After weighing in you will proceed to drive forward to go dump your load. After you dump your load, you will go back onto the scales to weigh out so that they can determine how much weight you dumped. Once they have determined total weight, they will tell you the final charge and you can pay appropriately and then leave the landfill.

Once you have visited the office, you will be directed to proceed to go dump your load. Most construction waste landfills have a few separate dump piles, depending on the type of waste you have, and what type of truck. You may have to drive a quarter mile or more and up or down hills to get to the correct pile in some cases, as landfills are often quite large. Typically there will be one pile that gets most of the waste and is not very specific, but there will usually be a separate pile for concrete and brick loads, and a separate pile for green waste like branches and grass. Typically you will back your vehicle up to the more generalized waste pile as will most other people. The landfill will typically have a spotter that works there and directs traffic and tells people where to dump. Make sure you pay attention to their directions. The landfill has a constantly changing landscape due to the large amount of trash that piles up over time. If you go to a transfer station instead of a landfill, after you check in at the gate, you will follow the path to a large covered concrete pad, and then follow the directions of the spotter to tell you where to back your vehicle up to dump.

Now that you're backed up to the pile to offload, how do you dump? Well, if you have a dump trailer, or a dump box, it's pretty simple, you just open your doors and press the button to dump then leave. But what about if you are not so fortunate? You can either hand unload, throwing all the waste out of your trailer by hand, or you could do what is called a pull-off. To do a pull-off, you place a pallet or tire at the front of your trailer BEFORE you fill it full of trash, and attach a chain to it. Once you fill it and go to the landfill, you can attach the other end of the chain to the bulldozer, and they will use power of the bulldozer to pull on the pallet and chain, dragging all of the trash out of your trailer with it. You then retrieve the pallet and chain for reuse. This is MUCH easier than doing a hand unload, but unfortunately, most landfills and transfer stations charge a little extra to perform this service. If you have a trailer full of construction waste though, you will quickly find out it's totally worth it. You can expect to pay $20-40 for each pull off. If you pay 2 men $12 an hour and it takes them 1hour to hand unload, you just spent $24 dollars, and have 2 disgruntled wore out workers that could be making money on a job rather than trying to save money. Now, if you can afford the financing it may be worth it to buy a dump trailer or dump box rather than paying for pull-offs. Consider that if you do 2 dumps per day 250 days a year, that's 500 pull-off charges. 500 x $25 per pull-off equals $12,500. You can add a dump box to a truck for $10,000 or buy a dump trailer for $8,000, and it will also shorten the time that you are at the landfill. That's over 100% ROI on your investment per year, so do it if you can finance it and/or have a big enough truck. If you are just starting off and need to hand unload despite my advice, make sure you bring a hard rake, a shovel, and a broom to get all the smaller stuff that is harder to do by hand.

Once you have off-loaded all your trash, you are free to drive off and leave if you are at a volume based landfill, or go back to the scales and pay if you are at a weight based landfill.

Landfill alternatives

Mulch Facilities

Mulch facilities are another major consideration when determining where to dump your load if you have branches, leaves, logs, or other "green waste". There are likely more mulch facilities in your general vicinity than landfills, making your logistics more efficient, they are typically cheaper than landfills, and it is the more responsible way to dispose of your waste anyway. Make sure that if you have a load of green waste that there is absolutely no regular trash or even treated wood. These facilities are very strict about not having contaminates in your load, not only because it lowers the quality of their mulch, but also because it can jam up their machines. Mulch sites will typically charge by volume to dump, but if you have a 16 ft trailer full of branches you may be able to pay $30-60 total. If you have thicker branches or logs, they typically charge more because it's harder to break these down. Not all mulch sites are equal price wise so make sure you shop around when you're not in a hurry to dump.

Scrap Metal

Scrap metal facilities will also be your friend. If you're not already familiar, scrap metal facilities are businesses that will actually buy your scrap metal from you for recycling into more metal products. You can dump just about anything metal at these places, like bikes, mowers, appliances, patio furniture, fridges, swing sets, file cabinets, copper, rims, BBQ pits, car parts, trampoline frames, etc, and actually get paid for it. At the time of the writing of this book, scrap steel is about 5 cents per a pound but in the past few years it has been between 3 and 12 cents per a pound. In other words, if you go unload a 16 ft trailer with about 2,000 pounds of scrap metal goods (pretty realistic load) at 5 cents a pound, the scrap metal place will give you $100 cash on the spot. When scrap is up to 12 cents per pound it would be $240, a little more exciting. It's important to note that you can get more money for rarer metals like aluminum (like 50 cents a pound), or copper ($3.00 per pound), and that these prices will fluctuate frequently as well depending on market conditions.

You need to recognize the fact that not all scrap metal businesses are equal. The most obvious distinction is the price that they will pay you per pound. At one point in time in Houston for example, a lot of the scrap metal places closer to downtown where trying to pay 4 cents per pound for scrap steel. Meanwhile, about 10 miles further northwest in Tomball another scrap place was paying 6 cents per pound. But another facility about 7 miles further northwest in Magnolia was paying 10 cents per pound. I hope this illustrates the fact that you need to call around because over time these differences can add up to thousands of dollars. What's crazy is that not all scrap metal facilities even accept scrap steel. Some of the smaller ones will only buy the rarer metals like copper and aluminum. Make sure you keep your more valuable metals separate from the scrap steel when it's convenient, so you can weigh it separately and get paid more.

Another distinction between scrap businesses is their size and corresponding unload techniques. The best scrap metal places are usually larger and have a large scale you can weigh your truck in and out on, and accordingly, have a large pile of scrap steel you can back up to and unload on, like a landfill. A lot of the smaller scrap facilities, however, want you to put everything you're getting rid of on a small 3 ft by 3 ft scale a little bit at a time, or into hoppers about as big a 2 wheel barrows. This makes offloading extremely inconvenient and time consuming, and also subjects your scrap to more scrutiny because they are handling it a little bit at a time. I don't go to the latter type.

Something that most scrap metal places have in common is that they have a few rules about items they won't take. They don't want metal that has a lot of other trash attached to it, but will accept a reasonable amount. For instance, if you have some aluminum window frames, they might expect you to break most of the glass off them, but if you have a metal porch swing with some cushions on it, they will let it slide. Scrap facilities also will expect that your items are free of oil, solvents, or chemicals. If you bring lawn mower or car engines, you will need to drain the oil, and if you bring a metal drum, it can't have any liquids in it for instance. If you are dropping off a refrigerant containing device such as a refrigerator or air conditioner, it is supposed to have all of the refrigerant and oil evacuated before hand by a professional. Most places don't enforce this rule, but it is something you should consider environmentally speaking.

It is a good idea to have a dedicated space for collecting scrap metal at your business facility. You will be hauling away a lot of metal and you will save thousands of dollars in dump fees and get paid thousands of dollars instead if you can separate it from your regular trash and store it until you get a trailer or two worth of metal to take to scrap. It's a good thing to do on a slow day if you don't have calls coming in but you need to keep workers busy. I wouldn't recommend spending too much time breaking down your scrap to extract the copper and aluminum to maximize the amount you get paid for scrap metal. You'll make more per hour by hauling trash; just keep the more valuable metals separate if it's quick and easy. Depending on scrap prices, the amount you get paid may account for as much as 4% of you revenue, and save you as much in dump fees. Some people even do scrap metal as their sole source of income and haul it off for free. Until scrap metal prices go back up to 10 cents per pound or more, however, I wouldn't recommend hauling any scrap steel for free. Some customers will assume that you will do it for free, or even pay them to take it, but I don't recommend accepting this as part of your business strategy.

Bricks/concrete/dirt/rocks/fill material

I'm not a big fan of hauling these materials in the junk removal business, but if you do, you may be able to dump them for cheap or even free. If you have clean fill dirt to dispose of, there are many people that will love to take it off your hands for free, so long as you are willing to deliver it. You can put an ad out on craigslist or post in a facebook group and you should get responses pretty quick. Some places that sell broken concrete want your concrete if it's clean (no rebar or metal) and may accept it for free. Note that the landfill will still likely expect you to pay to dump it. Some mulch places will also allow you to dump concrete or bricks for free because they use it as fill material, I would call ahead first though. If you have broken tile you may even be able to dump it for free if someone needs fill material on their property or needs a hard substance to use as a driveway. I've done these things before by putting ads up on craigslist. I was surprised by the amount of responses I got.

Used Lumber

There are lots of hobbyists or even contractors that would love to take unused, or used scrap lumber off your hands, if you are willing to deliver it, or even if they need to come to you sometimes. This is good for if you clean out a garage or shed and the customer has a lot of it, or if you remove a deck or fence and the wood is not really rotten. I've dumped trailer loads of deck material in yards of people I met through craigslist for free, rather than paying $100 or more. A lot of times it won't make logistical sense to try to coordinate dumping something for free with someone from craigslist, but if you've got more time than business or you're a baller on a budget just starting out, this is an option to consider. Craigslist people are annoying sometimes though unfortunately. Some people like to turn old fencing material into shelves and other furniture. I've talked to a fencing contractor before that used to bring his old fencing to a pallet place that would turn it into pallets.

Donations

A big part of the junk removal business involves cleaning out people's garages or homes where they actually have a lot of decent furniture, clothes, small appliances, tools, etc that are completely donatable or resalable. I prefer to sell most of this stuff myself, but if you don't have access to space to store this stuff until you can get it sold, you can always donate a large portion of it. There are lots of donation/charity places scattered throughout most large metropolitan areas, so sometimes it makes perfect logistical sense to drop by and donate some stuff on your way to the landfill so you can not only recycle some goods and help people out, but also save on dump fees. Some donation places are pickier than others, and you will likely have to separate a lot of stuff out and have some of it rejected by the donation people if it's a little too trashy, but over time this is still a viable strategy that can save you thousands of dollars per a year. If you have vinyl lettering or a truck wrap on your equipment, you can even pick up a few customers in the process. They will see you donating stuff to a good cause, trust you, and ask you to haul away their household junk or construction waste. True story, this has happened to me. It is important to note that a lot of donation places will not accept mattresses due to health and liability concerns.

There may also be donation places like Habitat for Humanity in your area that will accept remodeling goods like cabinets, sinks, wood, tile, shingles, appliances, or fixtures if they are new or in still usable condition.

Antique Shops/Broken Furniture/Pinterest

As serendipity would have it, I happened to live in a part of town that had a lot of antique shops when I first started my junk removal business. They would see the stuff I had in the back of my trailers when they would take a cigarette break in the alley behind their shops, and they started offering to buy it off of me. The cool part was that half the stuff they wanted was actually broken or needed work or refinishing, but as long as I sold it at a discount it was fine. I have sold literally thousands of dollars in broken antiques and broken antique/non-antique furniture after I got paid to take it away. The point is, if you have a place to store it temporarily, you can even save on dump fees and make money by selling certain items or furniture that needs work or is broken. People prefer hardwood furniture if you've got it, don't expect to resell screwed up particle board furniture. If you get enough stuff you might try contacting a few of these antique people or post ads on craigslist or facebook offering up items for refinishing or pinterest projects for sale. I personally have big "garage sales" frequently out of my warehouse on weekends, and I make sure to invite the antique shop people because a lot of them are serious buyers that will clear out a large portion of my stash.

Craigslist/Facebook

If you get some items that you don't feel like paying to dispose of, or the donation places are closed or won't take it, a lot of times you can give it away for free on craigslist or facebook. You'd be surprised at the relative crap that people will still want if you're willing to give it away for free. I wouldn't waste my time on small items this way, but giving away some bigger items may save you a little money on dump fees and make someone else's day. For instance, a mattress that has one little stain but is still relatively new, a couch that is a little too worn to sell but could still be a good garage couch, a wooden play set that you tore down but still has a lot of decent lumber and hardware, a broken riding mower that you don't feel like draining the oil out of, etc.

Obviously you can use craigslist and facebook to resell items individually. I personally prefer to only sell items that are worth $40 dollars or more this route, as it takes time to coordinate meeting up with someone or waiting on them to come buy an item. If you have big ticket items like refrigerators or furniture, or workout equipment, keep in mind that you will always be able to sell them quicker and for more money if you are willing to offer delivery. You can also post a no delivery price and a delivery included price separately. I won't go into too much detail on how to sell things on craigslist, but keep in mind that it will be one of your most important routs to resell used goods.

Garage Sales and Auction Sales

Garage sales are my favorite way to get rid of the good items that I get off jobs. If you have access to storage space in a garage or shop on your property you can turn some meaningful profits this way. Obviously you can sell furniture, tools, appliances, sporting goods, and other higher priced items this way, but don't forget to also keep the smaller items. You will be able collect MANY smaller items in your junk removal business, like clothes, shoes, cds, dvds, picture frames, books, even unopened shampoo and moisturizer bottles or opened cologne, that you can turn around and sell for $1-5 apiece. This may not seem like a big deal, but you can easily collect 300 or 400 of these items in a month and then make an extra quick $1,000 at your garage sale, and it gets people to stick around and start opening up their wallets at your sale because people don't really wince over shelling out a dollar or two at a time.

Make sure you put some real effort into promoting your garage sales. Post ads on craigslist, facebook, facebook beg borrow sell trade groups (lots of them), and put out stake signs at major intersections. Also consider making a contact list people can get on for your garage sales. People will be amazed by all the great deals you have and will ask you when your next sale is, so collect their name, email, and phone number so you can tell them. Another trick I do is to post single big ticket items that are at my garage sales individually on craigslist and facebook groups, and then write in my ad that they are free to stop by and check it out any time that day at the garage sale. Sometimes just posting an ad about a garage sale is too vague to motivate people to come. But, if you can laser focus their attention with one item they want, they may stop by, and then end up buying a lot of other stuff too.

You will probably need at least one helper at your sales, it can be quite a bit of work if you do it right. Remember that there is a cost to your sales though. You have to pay workers their hourly rate to separate out the good items and then pay for the storage space where you put these items, and then pay your workers wages when they help you at the garage sale and put everything back up that doesn't sell. If there is only a few dollars worth of resalable items off any particular job and it will be time consuming to dig out, sometimes its better just to head to the landfill with your goods and trash them. Similarly, if there is a large furniture item that won't sell for very much if it sells at all, sometimes its better just to dump it rather than have it take up valuable storage space. Also consider that your time is valuable and sometimes you stand to make more money just doing more junk removal jobs on a Saturday than having a garage sale. If you can go out and make $400 profit in a day on a Saturday hauling trash, as opposed to making $800 revenue at a garage sale minus labor for sorting, renting storage space, garage sale help labor (so more realistically a $550 profit at the garage sale), perhaps you would prefer to keep things simple and just haul junk.

Auction Houses/Estate Sale Companies/online auction

So what if you don't have a lot of storage space to hold onto things for resale, or don't feel like spending time on the weekends having garage sales instead of doing jobs? There is still a way to cash in on the good stuff you get, and that is to drop them off at an auction house. Some auction houses will be a little bit pickier about what kind of stuff they will sell for you, so you might have to call around, and you will not really be able to sell the small items either. But, you can sell the bigger things like hardwood furniture, appliances, tools, etc this way. Expect to pay about 30% of the total sales price to the auction house. The great part about working this way is that they should have a warehouse you can go drop a trailer load of goods at, and you can set reserves on your items. As long as you can store one trailer load worth at a time in your garage, or just rent a medium size storage unit, you can store your items until you can make a trip to the auction house logistically worth it. After they sell your items, they can just mail you a check, which should be itemized so you know you're not getting screwed. Sometimes you will get less than what you could get at a garage sale, sometimes you can get more. This is not a hypothetical method, I've done this before.

Of course, you can sell items on eBay as well. I wouldn't recommend selling anything less than $40 on eBay because I don't think the listing and shipping part of it would be worth it. I won't go into too much detail about selling on eBay because there is a plethora of resources addressing this on the internet already, but I do think it is important to mention their "eBay valet" program. You can ship many types of items to eBay valet for free (yes, they cover shipping) and have them take pictures, test items, and post them for sale for you and then ship them from their warehouse when they do sell. If they sell then eBay takes a percent of the sales price (20-40% depending on how much the item sells for), and if the item(s) don't sell they just ship them back to you, free. They request that your items be worth at least $40 resell value, and have a few restrictions on items they don't take. This is great for some name brand clothing you may encounter on jobs, as well as electronics. I've sold suits, purses, a storage unit of remote control helicopters, medical devices, and some other things this way.

Tires

I don't recommend taking more than 3 or 4 tires at a time, if you take them at all. A few tires at a time are not hard to dispose of. You should have many local tire shops in your area where you can dispose of them responsibly for a few dollars apiece ($2 a piece where I live). They will see to it that they are recycled properly. They will probably charge extra, like a buck or two, if it is still on the rim. Many of them won't take the tire if it is an 18-wheeler tire or large truck tire, so be cautious or charge more when taking the larger tires. Landfills will not take tires intact, because they can harbor mosquitoes and other pests, can pose a fire problem, and can pose an environmental problem. Most of them will take tires however, if you break them down. You can cut off the side walls and then flatten the remaining circular tread part by cutting it in half.

Be wary of taking large amounts of tires as a commercial waste hauler. There are state and federal regulations in place that require special permits, licenses, and insurance for transport, storage, and disposal of tires. Unless you are familiar with these regulations, don't haul loads of tires.

Paint/oil/solvents/other hazardous chemicals/compressed cylinders/refrigerants

Like with tires, there are significant regulations addressing the transport and disposal of paint. It is considered hazardous waste and you need to have DOT certification, and the correct insurances and licenses to transport it. To complicate things, it is very difficult to dispose of as well. Accordingly, DO NOT ACCEPT PAINT in your junk removal business. Similarly, there are many regulations concerning the transport of oil, solvents, and other hazardous chemicals, so DON'T ACCEPT THEM. Customers don't ever want to hear that, so when they persist just explain to them that it is illegal for you to take, and that they need to take it to their local city or county recycling center. Unfortunately, these government run recycling centers do not accept business produced hazardous waste, so you as a business will not be able to dispose there.

Depending on your jurisdiction, there may be one exception to the rule of not taking and transporting paint. In some cases, you can take latex based paint if the lid is off the can and the paint is COMPLETELY dried. In this case you can often dispose of it at the landfill without any issues. This does not apply to oil based paints, which take much longer to dry anyway. Hardware stores even sell a powder to help dry out leftover paint specifically for this purpose.

Even if you tell people you don't take paint, oil, or solvents, inevitably they will deliberately try to sneak them in, or it will accidentally end up in your trailer because it was in a box or bag that you didn't open, or they will claim that its dried out when it's not really all the way dry. For paint, when this occurs you have a few options. You can take off the lids of the paint cans and set them out to dry, you can pour the paint out to dry over something with lots of surface area, like used carpet you get of a job or used newspaper, or you can take it to a local recycling center. Recycling centers typically don't accept business waste however, because they are put in place and financed for ordinary residents of the local jurisdiction. Keep this in mind when deciding what vehicle to bring your paint there with if you get in a tight spot. If oil containers end up in your trailer, you can usually take it to your local auto parts stores and recycle it there. Oil you can recycle there includes not only your typical engine oil, but also hydraulic oil, transmission oil, power steering fluid, and brake fluid. Solvents can be dried out or burned, or recycled, but be very cautious and selective in the manner in which you evaporate them or burn them, as they can obviously very flammable.

Compressed cylinders used to store propane for grilling, or other gasses for welding, can pose another transport or disposal issue. If I end up with propane cylinders I typically just resell them at a discount at garage sales. You should not transport loads of flammable or compressed gasses without the proper permits. I have ended up with welding related cylinders before though, and you can actually sell them for a pretty penny if their inspection is current. If it is not, you may still be able to sell them at a discount, or offload them for free to someone on craigslist. At the very least, you can release the pressure and then remove the top and then dispose of them as scrap metal. The landfill does not accept compressed cylinders, which can be very dangerous around their heavy machinery. If you get fire extinguishers, half the time there will be no pressure left and you can unscrew the top and then dispose of them, otherwise, you can spray out the pressure and then do the same.

Cardboard/Plastic/Glass/Clothes/other basic recycling

The junk removal business at its core is essentially a logistics game. You make money off solving people's logistics problem. So a word of warning when it comes to recycling: the logistics of recycling junk are not always financially net positive, so be selective about what you recycle and when. Keep in mind that it takes time to sort out recyclable materials (paid labor) from regular trash, takes gas money and time to transport it to a disposal site, and takes time and rent to store recyclable materials if you want to collect them until you can make a recycling trip. For example, if you have a trailer full of cardboard boxes, it might be worth it to find a recycling facility nearby to dump it, and you'll save $50 on a dump fee. But if you have a trailer full of mixed trash, and it is a fourth of the way full with cardboard boxes that need to be dug out of the other trash, it may be more cost effective to just dump it with the other trash, because you would only be saving $10-15 on dump fees (if dumping by weight), but paying 2 guys to sort through trash for 15 minutes (not fun and cost $6 labor), then drive out of their way and dumping at an alternate location (30 minutes at least, another $12 labor plus gas), and while you're are losing a few dollars and time on this recycling proposition, you could be making money doing other jobs instead. There is an opportunity cost.

While recycling isn't always the most profitable thing to do, it is certainly the more responsible thing to do and is worth more in depth discussion. Probably the most accessible locations to recycle cardboard, paper, clothes, and some plastics will be school and church parking lots where they have the dumpster style recycling bins. Some businesses have them in their parking lots too, and some scrap metal places have started adding them as well. Even though many of these bins say they are for charity right on the bin, there are many people who don't realize that the companies that pick up these recyclable materials turn around and SELL them as feed stock for industrial production of similar materials. Meaning, the service is not costing the schools or churches money. I've actually had people call the cops on me while I was pulled up to recycling bins offloading cardboard and plastics at a school before heading to the landfill, accusing me of illegal dumping. The cop got a pretty good chuckle out of it when he came out and talked to me, and let me keep on doing what I was doing. I've also had other people at school parking lots drive up and try to tell me to stop recycling because they weren't sure I should be there. I hope this happens to you because it's hilarious and you can tell them to report you to the police for illegal recycling.

If you look up websites like www.recycle.net, you can find listings for companies buying and selling scrap recycled materials and what rate they're willing to pay for different quality and grades of the different types of materials. As a matter of fact, many of these materials are worth more than what scrap metal yards pay for scrap steel. For instance, many types of paper/cardboard can fetch $120-$300 per ton, and the same goes for many types of plastic. I wish I knew more about how the recycling business worked and more importantly the regulations involved, I would be inclined to set up shop myself. There are businesses that will buy batteries, compost and food waste, computers and electronics, glass, oils, paper, plastic, clothes, leather, wood products, and even tires (which many people view as an expense to get rid of) for use as feed stock for other products.

When recycling at the bins on schools, churches, and businesses, please be respectful of the rules they have posted on the bins. Don't put cardboard in the paper bin if they say not to, don't try to recycle Styrofoam because at the time of the writing of this book it is not acceptable as a recyclable plastic, be conscience of not recycling #3,5,6, or 7 plastics where prohibited, while #1, 2, and 4 plastics are usually acceptable (look on the label on the bottom of your product). Break down your cardboard boxes before throwing them into the bins.

In addition to recycling bins, if you're lucky you will have a larger recycling/sorting facility run by a company like Waste Management that is open to the public. These types of facilities will allow you to unload many types of paper, plastic, and cardboard, and sometimes glass and other materials. If your load is contaminated with other non-recyclable trash however, you will not be able to unload there unless you get permission before hand and you're unloading by hand and there is a very clear separation. At some facilities they will even pay you a small weight based fee for your recyclable materials, because remember, they are turning around and reselling them like a scrap metal yard. Some of these places will want you to have some kind of contract with them first though if they do pay out, and may only want larger waste haulers.

When it comes to clothes/textile recycling, if you're town is like Houston, there will be boxes placed all over parking lots for clothing donation. Don't worry too much about the quality or condition of the clothes that you dispose of in these boxes, because they aren't necessarily getting donated or resold at places like goodwill. Instead, the textile materials are being diverted to recycling centers and getting processed into other fabrics for rugs, mattresses, carpet, or any number of other things. They are getting paid based on weight for the clothes they resell to recyclers. On a side note, there are even some industrial recycling facilities that will take carpet and carpet padding, but unless you are close enough to the facility or have a carpet business, the logistics of the trip is probably not worth it.

Chances are you won't end up taking too many full trailer loads of glass, but if you do, you may be able to find a glass recycler in your area that will give you a few cents per a pound for it, rather than paying to dispose of it at a landfill.

Chapter 3: Junk Removal Job and Customer Types

The main different types of jobs and in depth discussion:

You could broadly categorize junk removal jobs into five main categories, each with subcategories:

1. Household items and furniture (often from people moving)
   a. All pre-moved to the garage or on driveway (my favorite type of job)
   b. All over the house, and sometimes back yard (a little more work, but worth it)
   c. In apartment complex or condo (way more difficult, charge more or avoid)
   d. In a storage unit (SO easy, and often resalable)
2. Construction Waste (boards, sheet rock, counters, cabinets, tile, fixtures, etc)
   a. In garage or on driveway (easiest location)
   b. On side yard
   c. In backyard (way more labor intensive, consider charging more, very common)
   d. Inside house and sometimes upstairs (no thank you, charge more, much more work)
   e. Heaps of tile, concrete, dirt, or mulch (I wouldn't do this without extra heavy equipment and extra charges.
3. One or two large items
   a. Upstairs furniture, difficult to maneuver through customers home obstacle course and heavy (typical big screen TV or reclining couch)
   b. Furniture or appliances downstairs or in garage, like couches, mattresses, desks (no big deal)
   c. Backyard items like trampolines, above ground pools, or BBQ pits
4. Demolition jobs
   a. Hot tub

b. Deck
c. Sheds (metal, wood, or plastic) and small buildings
d. Children's wooden play set/swing set
e. Inside demolition for investors (cabinets, carpet removal, counters, walls, toilet or tub removal, tile removal

5. Investor/Realtor/hoarder trash out jobs
   a. Large clean jobs with trash/furniture everywhere inside house, home still has a/c and was maintained
   b. Large nasty job with household items and furniture everywhere inside house, smells and has insect/rodent poop everywhere, house in abandoned state (charge more)
   c. Large job on a large property with stuff not only inside the house but spread all over the property outside. Not for the faint of heart, very time consuming.

1. Household items and furniture removal

Household items and furniture removals are the core of what junk removal companies are meant to take in my opinion. They are also the easiest junk removal jobs to perform and most profitable too. A large percentage of the time, when you are called out to do these types of jobs it's because your customer is moving in or out of a house, and they just don't have the time, patience, or inclination to deal with all the excess junk they have accumulated. There will usually be one or two large furniture items like a couch and mattress, and then random other things like tube TVs, outdated electronics, kids toys, dishes, clothes, lamps, empty and partially filled boxes and then a few random boards and garage items, etc. The list and variety of items you may end up removing is never ending in complexity. If the customer has already moved into their new home, the items are more likely to all be located in the garage or on the driveway of the new home. If they are moving out of the house you are cleaning, it is more likely to be spread throughout the home and your loading time may increase.

If everything is in the garage already, your crew should be able to load a 16 cubic within like 20 minutes. The further away items are from the loading point, longer it will take. If items are upstairs, in attics, or in a backyard, a 20 minute job can turn into a 90 minute or 2 hour job pretty easily. You will generally find much more resalable and/or donation type items if they are in the house or garage. Anytime you start removing items from the back yard, most of the time it will be complete trash.

It's kind of hard to go wrong with storage unit jobs as far as load time, because you can usually back right up to the storage unit and just toss everything into your truck. Loading times can increase dramatically however, if it is an indoors storage unit, even more so if it is indoors and upstairs. It takes a long time to get couches as well as lots of smaller items through doorways, down halls, into an elevator, back out the elevator then down another hall and through a door that might try to automatically lock you back out. This trouble applies to high-rise condo units, office buildings, and some apartment complexes as well. When you find yourself in this situation you should consider charging more. I personally refuse to do high-rise condos and multi-story office buildings because there is much easier money to be made elsewhere. People needing junk removed from these types of buildings will often ask about pricing BEFORE telling you what kind of building they are located in, sometimes deliberately hiding the fact and sometimes incidentally. Don't be afraid to discuss an increased rate, if they have called around they have probably figured out that it might cost more. To complicate things, condos, office buildings, and apartment complexes often present parking issues for large trucks or truck/trailer combos, especially if they are in a downtown area. This means you have to walk all that trash EVEN further.

Typical household item and furniture removal jobs can range anywhere from a quarter trailer (3 or 4 yards) up to a full trailer (16 yards) or more. On average these types of jobs will be about 8 or 10 yards, but there are lots of quarter full trailers and completely full trailers in between. Make sure you have some kind of minimum service charge in place in case people only have 2 or 3 yards of junk. You won't make any money if you're only going out and charging $50 at a time. The best kind of job in this category is a job that is just straight furniture. It takes very little time to load and takes up lots of space quickly.

2. Construction Waste

I personally abhor doing remodeling/construction waste jobs because it is a lot more labor intensive, harder on equipment, and more expensive to dump. I've considered turning down this type of work altogether, but it's just too common and profitable to run away from. It can easily account for 30%-50% of your revenue, and the jobs tend to be bigger (12-16 yards). I personally charge $30/cubic yard for c-waste (as opposed to the usual $25/yard for household), and sometimes tack on extra fees if it is in the back yard or far away from where I can park, and also if there is an excessive amount of tile. This price increase will bother a lot of customers, but let that be their problem if they don't understand how hard of work this is to be doing 2 or 3 times a day, sometimes in blistering heat or freezing temperatures. Because the dump fees for remodeling waste can be twice as expensive as regular trash on average, you need to approach these jobs with the mindset that you will be charging more. Loading times even if the waste is in the garage can still be an hour, and if it is in the backyard you can expect to spend 2.5 hours loading for a full trailer of boards and sheet rock. You will also need to be weary of stepping on or grabbing boards with nails.

For these types of jobs it is particularly more important to have the right loading tools. You can use a **garden cart/wagon** with large rubber tires to transport boards, sheet rock, and other large/long items from the back or side yard in increments of like 1 cubic yard at a time if you load it right. You can use a **wheel barrow** or **large trash can with wheels** to move a lot of the smaller items like cut up boards, roofing, tiles, etc from the back yard to your trailer quickly and efficiently. You should carry a **metal wide nose snow type shovel** in case you run into piles of tile or concrete, or other piles with small heavy bits and pieces. You can use a **stiff metal rake** to help pile up a lot of the smaller debris that you will inevitably run into.

Like I said before, either charge way more for a cubic yard or more of tile/concrete/roofing/dirt, or don't take on these jobs at all. On my website I tell people I charge $200 a cubic yard for these materials just so people won't bother me with it. If you're already on a remodeling waste job and you find a yard of tile, make them pay at least the extra $40 or so it will cost you to dump it, if not $80 or $100 more. Nobody ever wants to hear this, just be prepared to stand up for yourself and be clear with the customer BEFORE you begin loading it. Anytime you're getting questions about construction waste removal pricing over the phone, make sure you clarify over the phone BEFORE you schedule the job that they do or don't have tile/concrete and the like. If they do, they probably don't know or won't admit just how big the volume of this heavy debris is. Instead of asking them the volume, ask them how many square feet the tile or concrete used to cover, and deduce your own volume from there. Any more than 150 square ft of tile involved and you need to start up charging.

Another big consideration with construction waste in the yard is whether someone was smart enough to lay down a tarp. If they didn't, there may be a lot of small debris and boards embedded/crumbles/buried in the ground and your customer will be expecting you to still get rid of it. For tile/small boards/and other small debris with slightly larger debris this can be especially problematic because you can't get a shovel consistently underneath the piles, and you can't rake the piles, leaving you with the only other option of HAND EXCAVATION of these materials out of the yard. Make sure that if you encounter a situation where that might be expected, that you discuss that you don't do "hand excavation" or you at least charge extra, BEFORE you start the job. For most jobs this won't be an issue, but when it does a small bunny will die, a butterfly will lose its wings, and you will be fighting to not walk away from the job.

One more thing worth mentioning is pallet/crate jobs. There are a lot of potential customers that will call you wanting a large pile of pallets removed, but they won't want to pay your normal rates. This extends from the fact that there are a lot of people that will come pick up pallets for free to resell to pallet companies. Don't worry about trying to convince these people to pay your prices. Ask them if the pallets are in good condition, and if they aren't, just give them a take it or leave it type quote and move on. If they're in good condition do the same, but expect less of a positive response. Make sure people with crates know that you won't break the crates down for them free of charge so they can save space and thus money on dump fees. Just don't worry about losing out on these jobs, you'll just waste time and get frustrated.

3. **Single and two item jobs**

Typically these job will be a single couch, a fridge, or a couch and a love seat, a king mattress/box spring/frame, or a big screen TV. Sometimes these jobs are extremely easy and the item is already in the garage or downstairs or on the driveway, and you wouldn't even need two people to load it. About half the time however, the item is extremely heavy and/or upstairs that are possibly winding or split-level and there is a veritable obstacle course that your team will have to navigate to get the item out. In these instances it's not uncommon for the customer to actually need lots of trash removed, but only use your service to get the really difficult one. In other instances, they are using your service because they just bought a brand new version of the item you are hauling off, and don't know what to do with the original one.

When the items are in the backyard it is typically a barbecue pit, an old couch, a patio table, a trampoline, or sometimes an above ground pool. Be careful about quoting your service minimum charge on barbecue pits. Clarify whether it is a store bought BBQ pit on wheels or is it a custom made BBQ pit, which can be upwards of 400-800 pounds and have rusted out wheels. These monstrosities can be extremely difficult to move without cutting up with a torch or plasma cutter. I recommend just passing on these jobs altogether. People typically don't want to pay extra money to remove it, even if they recognize that it is more difficult. When there is a trampoline it will typically need to be disassembled, so consider charging a little extra for this, same with above ground pools.

Inevitably you will get calls about removing safes and pianos as well. I will often pass on these jobs altogether. There are whole businesses dedicated solely to moving these items because they can easily weigh 400 pounds and up, this is not YOUR business. If you're going to move a safe make sure you know what type it is and that it is below 300 pounds, and if you're going to remove a piano, make sure that it is at least downstairs and is an upright. Pianos, even upright pianos, are usually 450 pounds and up, and a lot of times the wheels are broken too.

When removing refrigerators and freezers, make sure you clarify that they are empty before agreeing to remove them. If not, at least charge extra to deal with the mess. Landfills cannot accept refrigeration devices because they contain hazardous refrigerants, and scrap yards won't accept a fridge or freezer with a bunch of rotten food like fish or deer meat, leaving you with no choice but to clean out all that maggot infested and mold sliming animal flesh yourself. Also, sometimes when taking out a fridge that is inside the house, you will have to remove the refrigerator doors, or door handles just to get it through the front door and/or other doorways. Alternatively, sometimes you can open the fridge doors and then angle it through the doorway upright, sliding it on a blanket or four wheel platform dolly.

For any type of single item job, you need to charge your order minimum, or more. This is the whole point of a service minimum charge. I personally charge a $75 minimum (plus tax), regardless of whether it's a fridge, a love seat, a couch, a TV, or even if someone just wants a plant gone. I will include up to 3 yards of trash for this price. Other major franchise junk removal companies operating in my area have even more expensive minimums, charging $85 and $120. I've even heard of another company operating in my area that has a $200 minimum. This may seem a little excessive for simply removing a couch, but it's actually barely profitable to charge $75 as a minimum. Let's break down the math as to why this is the case:

To remove a couch, I have to send out two workers to lift it and load it. It will take 30 minutes to get to the job, 30 minutes to get back to home base or another job or the landfill, and 10 minutes to park, talk to the customer, load the couch, get paid and leave, and that's if the customer is there on time or there is no traffic. That's 1hr 10 min for 2 men at $12/hr or $28 labor just to get the couch. Then, depending on where you dump it, it may cost $5-20 to dump it. Let's call it $5. Also, you have to pay workers to spend time dumping the couch at the landfill as part of a bigger load, which they probably had to combine the couch with, so add another $4 for the labor probably involved. Also, you have to pay for marketing just to get the job in the first place. If we are calling our marketing budget 10% of revenue, then this customer cost you $7.50 in pay per click, paying workers to post on facebook and craigslist, mini-billboards, vinyl lettering, website SEO, or however else you're marketing. In addition, you have to pay gas to get to and from the job and landfill, another $5 for your big truck. Also you had to pay someone to answer the phone, a few times as a matter of fact, just to get the job and filter out the other people asking question for jobs they didn't hire you for: another 10 minutes, or $2 in labor. Also factor in the insurance you pay every month, facility rental cost, and the equipment maintenance and prorated purchase costs: add another $10 (I believe that's a realistic prorated number). So $75-28-5-4-7.50-5-2-10= $14.50 in profit. $14.50 in profit would be fine if you could do 10 single item jobs a day, but the way people schedule things and how far apart your jobs are space over town, you likely won't be getting 10 single item jobs in a day. Now, if you charged something like $50 as a minimum fee, you would be losing money on every small job you did. So even though it may seem a little ridiculous to charge something like $120 for a company to remove a single item, possibly costing more than the item did cost itself to buy when it was purchased, it is the cost required to make a reasonable profit after considering the labor and overhead involved in a junk removal transaction. There is also an opportunity cost to scheduling small jobs when they might interfere with the ability to timely schedule a larger, much more profitable job. Junk removal is kind of a white glove service that the right customers are willing to pay considerably for, but only if you can do it on their terms and make it convenient for them.

4. Demolition Jobs

You may or may not choose to do demolition jobs in your junk removal business, but you will definitely get asked if you provide this service, so you may consider doing it. Keep in mind that to do demolition jobs you will need to bring extra tools to your jobs. You should be able to handle most demo jobs if you have a sledge hammer, large crow bar, smaller thin pry bar, a decent sawzall with wood and metal blades, a circular saw, power drill, wire cutter, and extension cords.

When pricing demolition jobs, people will most often want some kind of all inclusive flat rate quote. To estimate jobs I find that the most straight forward way is to guesstimate about how much volume the waste might take up and multiply that volume times my volume based rates, and then tack on an extra fee for the demolition aspect. For example, if I'm removing a 10x8 wooden shed, it might take up 8 cubic yards when broken down, so I multiply 8 cubic yards x $30/cubic yard for construction waste, then tack on another $100 or so for breaking it down, depending on how sturdy it looks. In this example, I would charge $240 plus $100, or $340 plus local sales and use tax. For the extra fee for breaking things down, you may just make up a price that feels comfortable for the particular job, or you can also approach the number more systematically by guessing how long it will take to break it down, and multiply that time by whatever you think your manpower's' hourly rate should be. For example, if it takes two men one hour to break down a shed, and you think demo work with tools is worth $50 per a man hour, then you would charge $100 for the demolition aspect of the job (2 man hours). After you get some experience, you will be able to quote many demo jobs pretty quickly. Be careful about quoting demo jobs from pictures, it's very easy to underestimate what it takes, or also overestimate and lose out on jobs. It's better to tell people that you can give them an estimate from pics or over phone, but your price is not firm until you see it in person.

One of the most common demolition jobs you may encounter is a hot tub removal. While hot tubs are delivered to customers' properties intact, it can be very difficult if not impossible to remove them all in one piece. Hot tub movers often require specialized dollies to lift and transport hot tubs into back yards, otherwise they require several men to lift and move them. Sometimes they even use cranes to get them in. During installation they may have to remove fencing and gates temporarily to get them through. After installation people often build other things like decks, gate ways, and fencing that will negate your ability to remove the hot tub intact even if you had the correct equipment or manpower. So, when you approach hot tub removals I recommend chopping it up into smaller, more transportable sections to get it done.

To remove a hot tub, first make sure that the hot tub electricity is turned off at the breaker, and then confirm that there is no electricity at the hot tub wires with an electrical tester. I usually then proceed to pry out the wood sides with a pry bar, sometimes bashing the sides with a sledge hammer if that's not easy enough. After that I like to cut out (sometimes pry and/or unbolt) the pumps/heater/electric box, which should now be accessible. Then you can take the sawzall, and using the wood blade (not metal, which is too fine), cut the hot tub body in half or quarters (or however small you feel like) so you can pick up the pieces and move them. If you can get the hot tub light enough to flip over, it often makes cutting it easier. If the hot tub has lots of water in the bottom left because the customer didn't drain it, you should be able to cut some of the tubing/piping near the bottom to make it drain out pretty quickly. Often times, the sawzall will have issues cutting the tubes that are routed around the hot tub (just vibrates on them because they are not firmly fixed). To circumvent this problem I like to carry branch shears to snip the tubes. The sawzall can easily cut through the PVC pipes, just not flexible plastic/rubber ones. After you cut the hot tub up and carry the pieces into your trailer, the wood base of the hot tub will probably be left intact, and it will likely be pretty rotten from moisture unless it's a relatively new hot tub. You can either cut the wood into carriable pieces with the sawzall, or break the pieces away at the joints with the sledge hammer. After you clear the hot tub, it is good form to cap off the wiring that went to the hot tub using large wire caps, just in case someone turns the electricity back on. When doing hot tub removals you should probably wear a dust mask or some kind of respiratory protection, as the fiber glass can get in your lungs and cause distress. Long sleeves and gloves may be helpful as well because it can make you itch. I typically charge $250-$300 for hot tub removal. If the hot tub is not completely above ground and is buried in any way, consider charging extra because these can be much more challenging to remove because you will have to dig out a lot of dirt from the sides.

Another common demo job is wooden deck removal. I typically charge $1.25 per a square foot for deck removal, not including concreted in posts. To remove decks I typically start by cutting the deck surface boards into 4ft or 5ft pieces using a circular saw or sawzall. After that you can use a long pry bar (3ft) to jam between the deck boards and pry the boards loose one at a time along each column. Use a still intact board to pry against to loosen the target board, and then work your way from outside to in one column of boards at a time. These 4ft boards should be easy to load on to your garden cart several at a time and transport to your truck. Once the surface boards are gone, there will typically be a frame of boards (2x6s or 2x8s) underneath, attached to 4x4 posts that have been concreted into the ground. You can cut the longer frame support boards with a sawzall, and then separate them from the 4x4 posts by hammering away from the 4x4s with a sledge hammer.

Once the support frame is gone, the posts will be left which may or may not be difficult to deal with, depending on how old and rotten the deck is. If they are rotten, you may be able to just give them a few good whacks on the side with the sledge hammer and they will break off at the concrete base. If they are not rotten, you can usually still whack them with the sledge hammer 7 or 8 times and they will break loose and be able to slide out from a cracked concrete base. After you remove the posts, you can either pull/or in some cases dig out the broken concrete base, or leave it there so that customers don't have a lot of holes in their newly reclaimed yard to fill. In a worse scenario, you will not be able to hammer out the 4x4 posts, and you will have to cut off the posts as level as you can with the concrete base using the sawzall. In the worst case scenario, you will not be able to hammer out the posts, and the customer will not want you to just cut them off at the base, and instead expect you to dig out the posts and concrete, which is a lot of hard and time consuming work. Make sure you discuss with the customer what they expect done with the concrete bases from the posts before you accept a deck job. I personally refuse to dig out the concrete from excessively concreted in hard to remove posts without an excessive fee for each post. Instead, try to sell them on the idea that if you take out all that concrete they will be left with several large holes in their yard which they will have to go back and fill in (which is actually quite true). Another issue that you will occasionally run into with deck removals is that some of the frame supports are bolted in to the concrete slab on the side of this house. In this instance you should be able to use a socket wrench to loosen the bolts and remove the board.

Sheds are another common demolition request. There are three basic types of sheds; plastic/Rubbermaid type sheds that snap together, metal sheds, and wooden sheds. Plastic sheds can simply snap apart and don't really require any effort to dismantle. Metal sheds are actually surprisingly easy to demo as well. All you have to do is go in with a metal (fine tooth) sawzall blade and chop off the roof by cutting around the sides of the perimeter at the top, then slice down the corners with the sawzall to separate the sides. The pieces will usually be relatively malleable and you can fold them and crumple them into carryable pieces. The flooring of metal sheds is usually the most annoying part to remove. It often consists of one or two layers of 4x8 sheets of plywood that rotted in the ground for several years, which will crumple slightly and be covered in insects when you pull them up. There will also usually be a 2x4 support frame, which will also be pretty rotten and come apart pretty easily. Sometimes the metal sheds will also have thin wooden boards along the walls as additional structural support, but these can be easily cut with a sawzall as well. It shouldn't take very long to dismantle a metal shed, so don't charge as much for demo as you would for a wooden shed. Think somewhere in the $100-200 range for metal shed removal.

The hardest sheds to demo are wooden sheds, especially if they have a raised roof with shingles, and if there are obstacles on one or more sides that prevent you from knocking the shed over or getting behind it. There is not really a single approach to dismantling wooden sheds that works best for all of them, as there are many different degrees of quality and craftsmanship. If there is electricity hooked up to the shed make sure it is turned off at the breaker before dismantling. Where applicable, I like to remove the siding of the shed first by hammering and prying outward, and then cut some of the 2x4s on the frame using a sawzall, enough to where I can just push the shed over and finish dismantling it on the ground. Other times, you may wish to cut around the perimeter at the top of the shed to loosen the roof, and then cut down the sides and the corners like on a metal shed. Sometimes if it has a shingled roof you might want to pry/pull off the shingles and throw them in a wheelbarrow or trashcan before moving the roofing because they add a lot of weight, and can also be difficult to cut through with a sawzall or circular saw. Sometimes the flooring can be very sturdy and hard to take apart if it isn't rotten, so you may want to use a circular saw or sawzall to cut through the plywood flooring, because 4x8s may be very difficult to pry up because of all the places they are nailed in. You can usually separate the joints of the wooden frame of the flooring (like with a deck) by sledging them apart. What some people call a shed can turn out to be a mini-house, so make sure you charge extra if there is sheet rock and insulation on the inside. In general, you may consider charging $300 for a 5x10 wooden shed, and $350-600 and up for an 8x10 or bigger. Once a wooden shed gets to be 10ftx15ft or bigger, you may want to start calling it a small house and turn down the job unless you have a skid steer, back hoe, or small excavator to tear it down with. These jobs get to be a little overbearing unless you have the right equipment, and people usually won't want to pay what its worth to have you take it down by hand anyway.

Children's' wooden swing sets/play sets are some of the easiest demo jobs to do. I typically charge between $250 and $300 to chop them up and haul them off. I like to sawzall the slide off, then cut the main support for the swings from the tower, then cut the ladder(s) from the sides and any other overhang supports. Sometimes you can just push the main tower part over right then if it is rotten enough, other times you have to cut more supports before you knock it over. Basically you just sawzall it in whatever way is convenient and makes the pieces small enough to carry, without cutting it to where it will fall on you. It's hard to cut through the chains on swings, so you will probably just want to unhook those from the main swing support beam. If you are feeling generous, you can usually save the slide and swings and other hardware and either give it away to someone who wants to make their own set and save money, or resell the hardware.

It's kind of funny, but I don't ever get many calls to demo wooden fencing, even though I get lots of calls to remove fencing that people or their contractors have taken down already and thrown in a pile. I think it is because cutting out fence panels is so easy people just do it themselves, and if they taking out fencing they are usually having a contractor installing new fencing right away, and the contractor will often times haul off the waste as well. The hard part is removing the 4x4 posts. If you do want to offer fencing demo, make sure you take into consideration how hard the post removal can be when you price it.

Another major category of demolition you may want to profit from is interior demo, taking out things like toilets, tubs, cabinets, counters, mirrors, vanities, carpet, sheet rock, fixtures, baseboards, wood paneling, doors, insulation, a/c units, tile, tile board, wood flooring, laminate flooring, showers, etc. When you quote these jobs, make sure you really take your time to consider how long it will take, and ALWAYS get your customer on a written contract detailing at least the scope of work to be performed, how much it will cost, and when and how it needs to paid. Customers have a tendency to misremember/lie/change their minds on things that you talk about when a job has any degree of complexity, and then act like it's all your fault if they don't like the results. They will also try to add more items without discussing additional payment, so make sure you are clear up front that changes to the work spelled out in the contract will incur extra costs and will require a "change order".

A lot of demo work like this will likely come from home investors who are fixing houses to flip or rent out, or less often from people who just bought a house and are fixing it up for themselves. I wouldn't accept any interior demo jobs that don't involve several items and instead only want one tub removed for instance, as most of the one item type people are cheap DIYs who won't want to pay enough to make it worth your while, and will be very picky and nosy about your work. Also, you may get requests from people that want you to remove cabinets or vanities but still leave them intact, just don't agree to that. There are too many variations of cabinet and vanity installations that don't allow you to promise to leave them intact, and as a matter of fact, you may also end up tearing up some of the walls and sheet rock that they are backed by. Tubs and showers are similar, sometimes the way they are installed require that some of the wall behind them will get damaged in the removal process. Exact methods on how to perform the various activities of interior demo is beyond the scope of this book, but there are a plethora of videos on YouTube showing good technique, and video is probably a more appropriate format for learning this anyway.

When pricing interior demolition, I like to determine what all the customer wants first, and then add up the volume on paper, then estimate about how many man hours it should take, and make up an hourly rate. Like other demo jobs, its comes out to be an equation of volume x rate/cubic yard + man hours x hourly rate. I recommend charging $30/cubic yard and at least $30/man hour, if not more for labor, at the time of this writing. If you end up charging $1000 or more to do a house, you are probably doing it right.

5. **Investor Trashouts/Hoarder Cleanouts**

These are some of the most financially enticing jobs upon first appearance because they have so much junk to remove, but that added revenue can come with great difficulty. These types of jobs typically come from home investors who bought a house to flip, or landlords who just evicted or lost a tenant, but also can come from family members of hoarders or a deceased loved one who was not a hoarder but still left a lot of stuff behind. There may be an entire house full of the usual furniture, dishes and food left in cabinets, a garage full of tools and junk, household items everywhere, an overgrown backyard with lots of boards and tires, an attic full of crumbling boxes covered in rat poop etc. When the job is big enough, usually people won't be okay with you just quoting a volume based rate over the phone, they will want you to come out and give a firm price.

You will probably get excited when you first see all the stuff to be removed, but if you quote all that stuff at your usual volume based rate you will quickly find that most people think that it's way too expensive, and either have unrealistic expectations of what things should cost, or are expecting a serious discount because of the size of the job, and the fact that they are serious home investors who may be able to bring a large amount of work to your business, but only if you give them a good price. Honestly half the time when you quote a job like this you are not really performing a serious quote, but rather donating your time to educate someone on how much it costs and what it takes to handle a large trash situation like this. It may be in some of these peoples best interest to rent a 40 yard roll off container or two and just have their friends and family load it instead. The other half of the time, the customer will try to get you to come down in price or move on and find someone to do it cheaper. So, the point is, be prepared to give some kind of discount or face rejection a little more than usual. That's not to say that jobs like this are impossible to get though, I've done my fair share of $2,000 jobs, and quoted jobs as high as $5,000, which I did not get.

You'll probably have more luck getting a big job if it tends to be a little grosser, like with rotten food in the kitchen, animal piss all over the carpet, rat or mouse excrement scattered throughout, blood stained mattresses, occasionally even stench left over from where there was a dead body because someone killed themselves, etc. If it is not a gross job, which many are not, consider only charging for removing the real trash, and then don't charge for the resalable/donatable which you can take and profit from another way. This is a more realistic way to hold on to home flipper clients who can bring repeat large jobs. When you get the larger jobs you can also add revenue by offering some of the interior demo services mentioned earlier, because these types of jobs are THE most likely type to require these types demo of services. You can also offer a deep clean service for this type of job; deep clean meaning you will scrub floors, toilets, tubs, baseboards, cabinets and wipe walls, and clean carpet and windows etc. Basically the type of cleaning people typically do when they are about to sell a house, and will pay $300 or more for.

Besides customers expecting discounts, there is another downside to really big jobs. Your employees are more likely to get wore out, need to take breaks, get frustrated, or get disgusted by all the gross stuff they encounter. You see, while most retail junk jobs may only last around an hour or less of loading time, followed by lots of driving where your workers can rest, the big hoarder type jobs can be a 2 or 3 day slug fest of loading loose trash and dirty furniture covered in dust and insects. The trash will also not all be located in the garage and boxed up, it will be all over the house and back yard and in the attic, and will thus require a longer loading time for the volume of junk there is. I've gone to jobs where I've filled a 24' U-Haul box truck 4 times. You'll be excited about making lots of money, but your employees will groan about all the nasty stuff they're about to have to touch, and you'll have more people calling in sick or making other excuses why they can't work that day. When you approach the large jobs, consider bringing in extra temporary labor for the job to make it go by quicker and easier, as long as you have the trucks to support the quicker flow of trash. If you don't have extra trucks/trailers, do like I do and rent a big U-Haul to improve your logistics. You can fit about 40 yards in a 24ft truck as opposed to a usual 16 yard trailer. Another important tool you will need to bring is a large trash can on wheels, one of the big ones that you can fit through doorways but can still fit a cubic yard or so of trash.

For the bigger jobs like this it's not a bad idea to get your customer under contract like with the demolition jobs. Hopefully one or two thousand dollars won't kill your business, but it is enough to hurt your business if someone doesn't pay. With a contract you can put a lien on their house and have recourse if they don't pay up.

Average Cubic Yard Measurements of Common Junk:

Couch: 2.5

Love seat: 1.5

Desk: 1

Fridge: 2

Dresser: 1

Recliner: 1

Overstuffed Chair: 1

Washer: 1

Dryer: 1

Dishwasher: 1

Armoire: 2

Piano: 1.5

BBQ pit: 1

Basketball Goal: 1

Shelf: 0.5

Computer Desk: 1

Treadmill: 1

Table: 0.5

Twin Mattress: 0.5

Full Mattress: 1

Queen Mattress: 1.5

King Mattress: 2

Bed frame: 0.5

Bedroom Carpet/padding: 1

Living room carpet/padding: 2

"Truck bed of trash": 4-5

Office chair: 0.5

1 car garage: 16

2 car garage: 20-32 or more

Hot tub: 6-8

Deck Boards: 4 yards per 100 square foot

Tub: 1

Tile: 1 yard per 300 square foot

Kitchen cabinets: 6-12

Door: 0.2

Bike: 0.2

There are also a few other distinctions you could make and ways to classify jobs:

Payment types:

1. Cash, check, or credit card in person transaction (obvious)
2. If customer is absent you can get payment via credit card over phone. I've done many jobs where I grab junk from the back yard, an open garage, or off the driveway, then send before and after pics to the customer and get their credit card via telephone once I'm done. Always process the credit card before you leave the job site, keep them honest.
3. Via invoice. I recommend only doing this if you have a contract with someone in writing or if you've established a relationship through previous jobs. Best for home flippers, realtors, banks or their property management companies. It may take some companies up to a month to pay you this way, and you will likely have to follow up occasionally because even the most reputable companies can "forget" to send a check, switch accountants, lose your invoice, etc. Trust me, it happens, even with people I know and trust.
4. Barter your services for goods or return services
5. Take items for free if they are actually good and resalable or as part of a bigger paid job. Be wary about offering to take items for free. Sometimes it's totally worth it, but most times people will pretend or think that their items have resell value but they really don't, and often times are dirty or slightly broken.

You can also classify customers:

1. Rich residential customer people that prefer convenience over money (my favorite, and most of my customer base). They are usual relaxed, flexible on scheduling, will throw away expensive stuff, and make you feel good about how much you

are helping them and that your prices are more than fair, even leaving tips.

2. Price conscience residential customer people who barely afford this kind of thing, and will put up some resistance or hesitate on price, and may even shop around but still call back and follow through. I don't mind these customers, it completely sensible.

3. Broke residential customer people who still want the service but are very price conscience. They will haggle and also sometimes deceive about the nature of the job, but still follow through a fraction of the time. They also seem to be more demanding in terms of extra service they want for free (light demo or breaking down boxes and wooden furniture to save space), and also seem to want things done last minute and are inflexible on the time. To top it off, a lot of these people won't even be in your service area to begin with because they didn't check your service area. I can't be too judgmental on poor people because I have been one, but it seriously makes me contemplate the planning ability and forethought of poor people, and general functioning and health of their prefrontal cortex. A lot of these customers will come from craigslist posts, but craigslist does generate some great jobs, so take the good with the bad.

4. Broke people who want the world delivered but don't want to pay for it. Straight up they will call and ask you if you will pick up their broken appliance or ripped up dander covered couch for free because it might be worth something to somebody.

5. Would be customers that have a truck or trailer all loaded up and would dump it themselves if they just knew where. I'm always willing to help people who are willing to help themselves and hopefully you are too, so don't be shy about telling them where the best and cheapest landfills are in your area, and other creative ways they can dispose of their trash.

6. Contractors (good and bad). Most remodeling type contractors will haul their own waste from jobs or rent a roll-

off container. If they get in a bind or are short on time they may revert to your services. Most of the time it's an honest remodeling waste job, but other times they are clearly just trying to pass on a terrible job they don't want to do themselves, and underpay you for it, and sometimes even take advantage of you even you don't know the right questions to ask. Always ask if there is much tile, brick, or mortar and ask where the waste is located to help screen the bad ones out. Always get paid before you leave the job and don't let them say they will get back to you with a credit card. As a matter of fact, if they say there is a little concrete or tile but it's covered by boards, lift up some of those boards and check before you start the job because sometimes a little is a lot. Let them know up front that if they didn't lay down a tarp you will NOT hand excavate materials out of the dirt.

7. Landlords and evictors. These are great customers because they have bigger than usual jobs, usually the house isn't in a terrible state of repair, and they see the service as a cost of doing business and are ready to play ball. If they try to act like you should give them a good price because they can bring you lots of business, ask them how many houses they own. If they only own 2 or 3 they are not really a big deal. If they own 10 or more MAYBE give a discount. If they own 50 or more, they probably already have their own property maintenance company or handy man that handles this stuff at a discount rate, and probably won't call you in the first place.

8. Home investor types with big jobs. They are great but may haggle a little bit. If they want to haggle make sure you ask them how many houses they own or how many they flip a year. If it's only 3 or 4 a year, they are not really worth a discount. I work with a company that does 50+ a year and I still only get one trash out a month on average or less from them. Remember that your profit margin is about 20% and your advertising budget is about 10%. So if you have repeat business it might be worth at least a 10% discount, but I

wouldn't drop it more than 20% in price as a general rule. Sometimes the logistics and economy of scale skew the number a little on simple price drop calculations for a big job, just remember that you could always advertise more and get more jobs that are easier where you don't have to drop your price.

9. Apartment/Condo managers and property management companies. These people usually have their own in house property maintenance workers who take care of trash and junk removal, and have dumpsters on the property where they can throw the stuff away too. If they call you it's probably because they are having problems with their usual workers and or the complex recently changed owners or managers. If you do a job for them they will want to be invoiced, and want a discount rate, and may complain about it later. That's not to say that you won't get some good repeat business from those potential customers though. I had a 300 unit apartment complex for disabled veterans who worked out a deal with me to haul off all the furniture people threw out by their regular dumpster (which does not accept and cannot accept furniture because it is too bulky and is "non-compressible waste"). It was probably difficult for them to get a roll-off dumpster at the same complex due space concerns, increased city regulations and fire codes (it was downtown) which drive up the price and company insurance requirements on both sides of the transaction. So instead they had me come out once or twice a month and clear they area of mattresses, desks, sofas, TVs, etc, and also break down the wood furniture, and probably actually saved a little money that way over the alternative. Later I dropped them as a customer because they were "forgetting" and taking too long to pay invoices, something I hear a lot of property management companies end up doing, so watch out. If you do work for property maintenance companies as a subcontractor at a discount rate for the promise of higher

volume business, just make sure you don't go TOO cheap. Remember, this is a business you are running, and if you do lots of work for a cheap rate your really just turning your business into an over glorified job. JOB is a dirty four lettered word, right?

10. Waste hauling brokers. There aren't too many businesses that are truly "brokers" of junk removal services. Usually they just broker roll-off dumpsters, porta-potties, fencing, and other services that are more easily quantified for a price mark up upon brokering a deal. Occasionally you will get contacted by a waste removal broker who can send you pictures of a job in your area and ask for a quote, but unless you give some stupid low price you probably won't get the job because those people are shopping around for cheap prices, and require their customer approval on top of that. Home advisor and Angie's List are almost acting as brokers, but instead charging you for leads that may or may not pan out.

11. Random businesses. Sometimes you will get calls from a retail or furniture store that went out of business, a warehouse based business, or any type of office based business. These jobs can be big and profitable, just watch out for poor parking situations in office buildings, and if a retail store or resell shop wants a discount because they think the stuff is resalable let them keep shopping if they don't want to pay full price. If the stuff was that good that would have sold it or donated it already.

12. Storage Unit Businesses. I've have some repeat customers that own and manage storage unit complexes, but most of them have employees that will handle trash removal situations and/or have figured out that it may be cheaper to rent a roll-off container sometimes. Consider giving some type of discounts to these customers if they are the operators of the business (not the space rental tenant customers). They may also refer you to their tenants who need to clear out units when they are moving.

13. Looky Lous and time wasters. Unfortunately, you are going to get a TON of calls from people who just want to know more about your services and how much they cost. It is part of your job to educate the general public on junk removal services and pricing, and even though you will be taking inbound calls from people that want your service, you still need to SELL them on it and find ways to close the transaction. Even if you're the best salesperson in the world however, you will still not be able close on every call. In fact, most of your callers will not commit to a job, they may be in just research phase, or aren't sure when to schedule, or need permission, or are too broke to afford you etc, so don't take it personally.

14. Friends and family – by far the worst type of customer. They don't want to pay full price, will have you doing jobs you wouldn't normally accept, and drive to places you don't normally go to, at off business our times, then recommend you to their friend you don't know who are even worse and cheap but you don't want to offend because it might come back to you. Avoid doing these jobs for anyone you wouldn't do it for free anyway.

15. Foreigners. They can be great customers and are often quite affluent as well. At other times they can be very difficult to communicate with via telephone because of their accent and broken English, and at the same time haggle unabashedly because that may be their cultural norm. As a general rule if I can't understand someone on the phone, I find an excuse to not do business with them pretty quickly and get off the phone.

Chapter 4: Marketing

Marketing

If you are good at marketing and sales, the rest of this business will work itself out. If you don't have calls coming in, it won't matter how good you are at doing everything else, so let's learn how to make that phone ring! Let's start off with some basic steps and then get into detail on each.

1. Set up a phone number for your business
2. Make a website and do basic SEO
3. Make a Google plus page and Google mybusiness page
4. Make a business facebook page and also a personal page if you don't already have one
5. Join all your local facebook beg, borrow, buy, sell groups so you can post ads later
6. Create a craigslist account and start posting ads, even if you don't have a business going yet
7. Create a Google adwords account and a bing account
8. Rent some mini-billboards
9. Put vinyl lettering and signage on your trucks and trailers, or sign magnets at the very least
10. Have business cards made
11. Drop business cards at all local storage unit complexes, as well as realtors' offices. Call local home investors, flippers, and landlords. Network!
12. Tell everyone you know you are starting a junk removal business
13. Start doing PPC on adwords, Bing, and facebook, and posting your services to facebook groups.
14. SEO, SEO, SEO: twitter, pinterest, blogging, facebook posts, videos, etc.
15. There are lots of other marketing tools that I don't necessarily employ or recommend, but I will tell you the pros and cons of

some of them, as well as tell you about some of the marketing efforts I've made that didn't really seem to work out.

16. Keep your customers happy enough to be repeat customers, but only if they are profitable customers. Repeat business should be considered another form of marketing.

Setting up a phone number

I'm assuming you already have a cell phone, but I don't think it's a good idea to have all your business directed permanently to your personal number. So, either get another phone and corresponding phone number to use for business, and/or get an account with an online call transfer/tracking service such as callrail.com or ringcentral.com. The latter is what I do and I suggest you do the same. If you aren't sure what these call transfer services do, as I wasn't, I'll explain. Rather than posting your real phone number to your advertising or business cards, you can pick another phone number and have any calls routed through the transfer service to your real phone number, but also be able to filter/record/track the calls and add a call menu or recorded message along the way. You can also have as many different phone numbers as you could possibly want, and route them to whatever phone numbers you chose, at different times and at different situations if you want.

For example, I personally have a callrail.com account and pay $33 a month for 11 different phone numbers which all route to my original cell phone # that I have on me at work at all times. I have one number for facebook, one for billboards, one for my main website, one for Google adwords, three for different craigslist accounts, and the rest for 3 other websites I have and other marketing ideas I always seem to be experimenting with. Anytime someone calls the message is recorded online, the source is recorded, and I get a message before the call is transferred when I pick up telling me what the source is. In the past I've also put in an interactive call menu (dial 1 for this, or 2 for that) which I did away with later, and also redirected messages to voicemail after certain hours. You can also set the phone to ring more than one number at once and transfer to whichever one picks up first, or do a round robin that rings to different phone #s one at a time until one picks up, etc. The point is there is lots of cool stuff you can do, and it's nice to separate your personal life from your business, so don't use your personal number, set up a call transfer account instead. If you want to get real fancy you can also set up a vanity number that is toll free like 1800-GOT-JUNK did, but the better numbers might be a little more expensive to buy or unavailable, everything else is pretty cheap and reasonable. It may be a good way to separate yourself from the competition by looking more professional.

Make a website and do SEO

Websites are so common now days that you should be able to have one made for a few hundred bucks, or even set one up yourself using the basic user friendly tools on sites like wix.com or hostgator.com. If you have one made professionally, make sure you outline exactly what you want to say on each page (write it out), and what types of picture you want to put on it. Web designers are not mind readers; they design the format, layout, and graphics of websites. You will need to buy a domain name (register a .com like atlantajunkdudes.com that isn't taken already), and then design the site and pay for hosting to get it on the web, all of which I recommend be done at hostgator.com, and you can pay less than $20/month to keep it up on kicking. Their web design tool "weebly" makes the design aspect pretty idiot proof for a beginner, I should know, I've done it. I don't get a kick back or anything for saying that, I'm just trying to give you a firm direction if you don't know what you're doing and can't afford to hire someone who does. Make sure you use their basic SEO tools and fill in all the blanks so all the major web browsers like Google and yahoo can crawl your website and index it correctly. Good SEO techniques are beyond the scope of this book and are the subject of hundreds of thousands of free articles online.

Check out your competitors websites online and decide which elements from those sites you do or don't want to include in your own. I think some major topics you need to address on your website are: what kind of stuff you take, how your service and pricing works and any extra services you offer, what your service area is, what your phone number is (on every page), pictures of your equipment and crew working (make it personal if you can), how to contact you, and an online form people can fill out to request junk removal service and/or pricing. If you are upfront about pricing and rates, makes sure its spelled out on your website, if you just want to give quotes in person only, focus less on pricing issues and instead on why and how you provide the best service.

Once your website is up and running, make sure you submit it to the major search engines for indexing. While you're on Google, go ahead and make a Google plus page and make a Google business page (just follow directions online to learn how). This will allow you to rank better on Google, as well as show up on maps and in local searches on Google when people are looking for trash removal in your area. Getting ranked higher on Google search can require a lot of good search engine optimization, a service you may have to pay someone to perform if you really want to show up on the first page in your general area. You can still rank decent for the local searches based on peoples IP addresses in your area in the maps for businesses near you even if your SEO is not the greatest. For example, I show up first on Google for Tomball Texas, and on the maps as well, but not Houston overall, which is my target market. Having good page rank through superior SEO can really make your business soar, and I will tell you some ways to increase your SEO, but national junk removal companies spend thousands and thousands of dollars and hire experts to rank at the top, so edging yourself up there to the first page in a major metropolitan area can be quite difficult and competitive.

Make Facebook accounts

You need to have at least two different facebook pages, one for a personal facebook page and another strictly business page (local business). Set up your business page on facebook and just follow the instructions they give you, adding lots of photos of you and your crew doing jobs and your equipment, your phone number, service area, etc. After that set up a personal page if you don't already have one. You will use this page for posting ads on facebook groups later. You can't post ads with a business account page, so don't name the personal account page after your business. While you're on facebook, go ahead and start investigating their paid advertising options and open the advertising account with a credit card so that you can do paid advertising later when you're ready.

Post to facebook groups for free!

Now that you have your website and facebook pages up and running, start taking advantage of some of the local facebook groups that allow you to make business postings. Most of them will allow you to post any day of the week and not flag you for spam, but some will only allow you to post certain days of the week, if at all. You will have to read the rules in the "pinned post" to make sure you are in compliance, or if they even allow local business ads. My wife does most of the posting to these groups for the business through her personal facebook account, and is a member of close to 100 groups in the greater Houston area. When searching for these groups to join, search for terms like "beg, borrow, buy, sell, trade" and then your local point of reference like a city name, neighborhood name, HOA name, or highway name. Also search for groups related to real estate investing, wholesaling, homes for rent or sale, etc. This may be a way for you to get connected to real estate investors and realtors. Every Monday my wife spends about an hour pasting ads to the different groups she has joined, and I guarantee the effort pays off because I get a few jobs a week at least off facebook, and many more calls.

Using Craigslist.com

Go to Craigslist.com and set up an account if you don't already have one. You will need to perform an email verification step as well as a phone verification step. It helps if you can receive text messages for this phone verification step. Once you have an account set up (which is free if you didn't already know), you can start posting ads to the service section and for sale section for junk removal. Appropriate service sections where you should not get flagged include "labor and moving, household services, farm and garden, small biz ads, real estate services, and skilled trade services". You can also get away with posting some junk removal ads in the "for sale" section under "general for sale". I typically post the price as $1 and then detail prices in the description. I think a lot of people accidentally search for services in the "for sale" section, because that's the search box that automatically pops up to begin with on craigslist. When posting, look at your competitors ads to get a feel for the elements you might like to include in your own, and figure out what sounds professional and competitive. I tend to write "Junk and Trash Removal" and locations like "Spring, Cypress, NW Houston" in the title, then detail the junk removal prices, how the service works, service area, and phone number in the description. Many people think it's important to know that you are local if you are in a big area like I am in Houston. Sometimes you may want to mix it up and not put very much detail in your ads so you have the opportunity to get people on the phone and really sell them if they're just calling around price shopping and information gathering.

In an effort to eliminate spam, but still allow local businesses to have some access, craigslist has created some spam policies that you need to adhere to if you want your posts to show up. There are also some games that your competitors and disgruntled people on craigslist like to play that can disrupt your craigslist advertising. First of all, at the time of this writing, you are only allowed to create one craigslist account per IP address per phone number. If you try to create multiple accounts with one phone number or IP address, you won't be able to. Also, you are only allowed one active post per a service section at any one time, which you can renew every 48 hours. This post will expire every month, but you can delete it and repost when it does. You can have multiple posts in the for sale section, just make sure they are not identical to each other because they may be flagged as spam. I suggest you download a craigslist app on your phone that can automatically log you into your account, and renew your ads in the morning every day when they are available for renewal.

If you try to violate these anti-spam rules, craigslist may automatically delete and or flag your posts that are in violation, or may also "ghost" your account or posts. Ghosting posts means they will appear to be active to you, but really only show up on craigslist to your IP address, and anyone else on craigslist will not be able to see them. Basically its craigslist way of allowing you to punish yourself for spamming by allowing you to waste your time posting and renewing and verifying ads that won't show up. There are definitely ways around craigslist's anti-spam measures and you will likely see your competitors totally gaming craigslist, and drowning out your ads with all theirs. It definitely happens to me every day. One way is to get your friends or family to create accounts on their own computers with their own phone numbers and emails, and then give you the password so you can post ads, and just use a picture that includes the correct phone number so people can reach you instead of the phone number of the account used to create the post. There are also professional craigslist ad posting services that charge a dollar or less per ad and use their own techniques and equipment to make sure they can spam craigslist. If you set up a virtual private network on a proxy server that you rent from someone else, you can basically act like you have another IP address in eyes of craigslist and post more ads that way. I'm sure there's lots of ways to do it, but it's really beyond what I can tell you.

Sometimes if a competitor sees your ads and they don't want the competition they may decide to flag you and your ad will be deleted from craigslist as inappropriate even if it is legitimate. New ads are much more vulnerable to flagging than older recently renewed ads. Craigslist has an algorithm where if new ads are flagged by users they can be taken down, but if an ad has enough views without flags, or a high enough percentage of views without flagging, even if someone does flag the post later it will leave it up. Accordingly, some articles recommend that when craigslist sends you an email with a link to your ad telling you that your post was successful and is active, you should click that link several times so that it counts as unflagged views and reduces the likely hood of it being illegitimately flagged and taken down.

I actually started my own junk removal business through free ad posts on Craigslist, eventually graduating to more sophisticated forms of advertising. I posted my first tester ad one October and got a call from a contractor within 30 or 40 minutes of posting it. I made a quick $80 for about 30 minutes or less of work, and have been sold on this business ever since. I don't think you should try to run a business solely from Craigslist leads, but you can definitely get some business from Craigslist.

Paid advertising on Google Adwords, Bing, and Facebook

These three advertising sources are a very important part of the type of marketing I recommend. Not only do I use Adwords, Bing, and Facebook paid advertising, but most of the national franchises as well as some of my more local competitors do as well. I can guarantee you that the big companies are not dropping the kind of money that they do on this without having crunched the numbers and determining that it works and is profitable. Doing PPC (pay per click), CPM banner ads, and video advertising correctly and profitably is the subject of hundreds or thousands of books, articles, videos and websites, as well as the core focus of many business to business advertising agencies that get paid big money to set it up an ad campaign and operate it correctly. I will outline some of the basics as they apply to junk removal advertising, and hopefully it will be enough to get you started.

A large part of my advertising budget is spent on Google Adwords Pay Per Click advertising alone. To set up an Adwords account, go to Google.com and type in "Google Adwords sign up" and then follow the links and prompts to set it up. Or, if you have the money, hire a professional to do it for you. You will need to create a login and password, put a credit card on file with them to pay for it, and have a website up already so that the PPC ads and other advertising has a website to send customers to. Once you create and verify your account you will need to make a new campaign and enter the parameters of your ad campaign(s). Here are some examples if the type of info you will enter.

Some relevant considerations:

Type: Search Network only. This means you are showing ads only to people actively typing in search terms. Not on apps or display ads on other websites.

Networks: Google search; search partners. . This means you are showing ads only to people actively typing in search terms. Your PPC ads are not showing up on random other websites that might try to game Google's PPC system to get ad revenue. There are other options, but this is a basic one that you can't go wrong with.

Devices: All. This means your ads will show up not only on PCs, but laptops, mobile phones, and tablets as well. You want to show up everywhere, because customers search for services using all types of computers.

Locations: These are the zip codes/cities/counties in which your ads will show up. Google tracks peoples IP addresses and can use this as a way to target your ads to the correct geographical regions. I prefer to use zip codes to target my ads, because I can target wealthier zip codes in my service area where people have more money to blow. You also have the option of selecting cities, or a radius around particular cities. Again, I think zip codes are the best way to go.

Location options: Target. Select people in my target location.

Exclude. As a money saving safety measure, you can specifically exclude certain locations, or search terms related to certain locations. Consider excluding poorer areas or more dangerous areas.

Languages: I always just select English, but if you know other languages that pertain to your service area you could probably get cheaper ads because there is most likely less competition for advertising in the non-native dialect.

Bid Strategy: Manual CPC. I like to control my own rate for what I'm willing to pay for CPC so I select this option. There is another option where Google will set the rate for you to optimize your ad rank, but I see the possibility of this method starting bidding wars that get out of control in Google's favor.

Budget: This is where you set the max budget you are willing/wanting to spend per a day on a particular adwords campaign. For instance, you could set $27/day and if you show ads 30 days a month you would end up spending close to $810/month on CPC ads on Google adwords. You can expect to spend $5 or $6 per click, so don't expect much results from your CPC campaign if you only set like a $5 or $10 a day budget. Instead, expect to drop $800 or more a month on adwords and you might get a job every day or every other day from a click that converts to a call and a sale. It may seem terrible to spend something like $35 in CPC just to get a job, but I've gotten jobs worth as much as $2400 from one $5 click on adwords. I've also gotten single item jobs (not very profitable) that gained me a repeat customer who later used my company to do a job in the $1000 range. The math on marketing is not always straight forward, but if you average out your results over time, I think you can use the adwords CPC game to your financial benefit.

Schedule: Adwords allows you to select which days of the week you want your ads to show up, as well as which time slots/hours on those days. You can also pick starting and ending dates for your campaigns. I advertise pretty much every day, from about 7am to 8:30 pm, basically the times I am willing to answer the phone and try to convert a sale. In the past I've turned off ads on Sundays and late Saturdays. Landfills are typically closed during those times and you can quickly be put in the situation of having a customer, but having no place to put their trash. Furthermore, customers who call during these times are typically high maintenance, poor planning customers, who are additionally somewhat cheap and waited till the last minute to take care of their overwhelming trash situation. I don't like dealing with these people, nor do I like working Sundays. I am weary of advertising at times that are not my main business hours because if people can't pick up my phone and call me after reviewing my website, I can't convert that sale and serve an immediate need, and my conversions from CPC probably drop. Conversely, however, you need to consider that sometimes people do research weeks or months in advance of needing your service, so you constantly want to advertise to keep those potential customers in your sales funnel. Weigh your options and do what works for you personally.

Ad delivery: When you are first starting out your campaign, you might want to select "rotate indefinitely" to swap out your ads and see which kind of ad copy is working best for you. You can then make more informed decisions about which ads are worded best and get better click through rate and show those more often. You also have the option of letting Google optimizing your ad rotation for you, and show the ads that are converting best more often.

Once you have set your campaign settings, you will need to set up adgroups for the specific campaign (groups of ads and keywords for specific marketing goals), enter keywords you want to target for the adgroup(s), and write the ads that show up Here are some example screen shots of what you will end up with for adgroups, keywords, and ads:

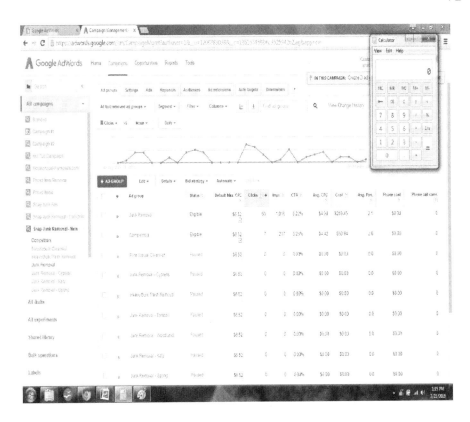

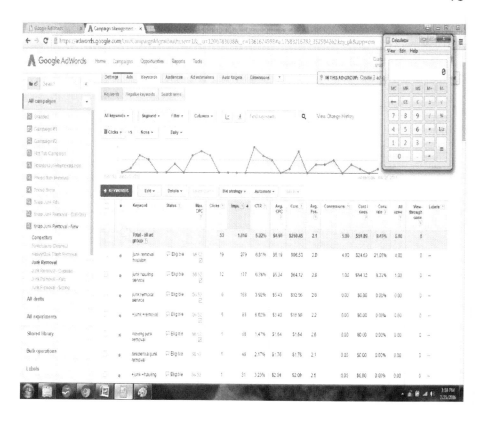

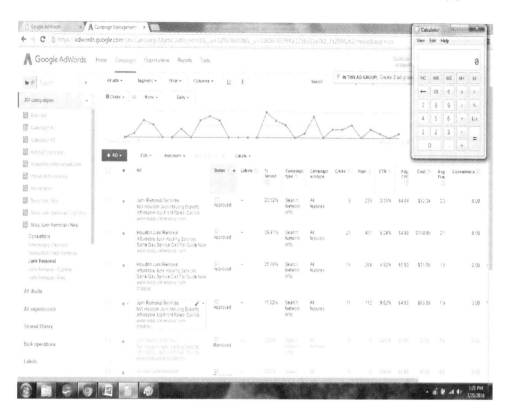

Some additional considerations for keywords you want to target, ad copy, and successful adwords metrics:

Keywords:

I find that the broader the keywords you target for junk removal are, the more realistic your campaign will be. Unless you're setting up a national company, which if you are reading this book I hope you're not jumping to that point just yet, many of the more specific search terms you may dream up for junk removal advertising will not have enough search volume, and adwords will pause your ads for those keywords because there is not enough people searching for those terms on a daily basis. For instance, I can get clicks for "Houston junk removal" every day all day, but if I enter in keywords that are much more targeted geographically, like

"Pinehurst junk removal", my ads will not end up showing up because not many people will type that search term. This non-specific keyword scenario will run contrary to what many CPC gurus will advise you to do in general, but there is a time and a place for more advanced CPC techniques that are really beyond the scope of this book.

Another consideration is that some search terms, while related to junk removal, will give you very poor quality leads that don't convert well. For instance, I tried CPC for "trash service" before, but instead of getting bulk junk removal requests, I got calls from people asking if I am the weekly trash service provider in their area, and why hasn't their trash been picked up yet, etc. Also, you might consider advertising for specific item removal, like "couch removal" or "fridge removal", but if you do this you will end up with leads calling you that really only have just that one item to remove, and these small jobs are not very profitable.

As mentioned before, clicks will often cost you between $4-$6 dollars for junk removal related keywords, with the better keywords having more competition from national chains. The higher cost is also associated with a better ad position (near the top on the right side of the screen, or at the top center of the screen before the usual real search results. I try to bid my ads to stay between positions 1 and 3, and have a max bid for most search terms set at $6.52. If you can get a click through rate (CTR) of around 5% or better, you probably have a healthy keyword selection, and decent ad copy for those keywords. 1% CTR is a little low, and anything above 5% is pretty fantastic, in my opinion. I'm sure some CPC experts would cringe at some of the things I'm saying here, but I'm a junk removal expert, not a computer whiz.

When adding keywords to your campaign, you can also ad search modifiers like +s or " "s or [] or parenthesis to have even more control of what search terms your ads appear for.

I think this section on adwords CPC would be incomplete without giving you some actual search terms you can use when first starting your campaign. Keep in mind that you will want to tweak your campaign later to optimize it, and that my geographically targeted words will not be appropriate for your area (enter your own city in lieu of "Houston"):

Junk removal Houston

Trash pick up

Trash pickup

Junk hauling service

Junk removal service

Junk removal

Moving junk removal

Residential junk removal

Junk hauling

Cheap junk removal

Junk services Houston

1 800 junk

Junk king

College hunks haul junk

Writing the CPC ads:

Here is an example ad I use for my business:

Junk Removal Services
NW Houston Junk Hauling Experts.
Affordable, Up-Front Rates. Call Us
www.mywebsitewhichi'mnotputtinginthisbookpleasedon'tcallmewithquestions.com

It is standard to have your website name at the bottom. Notice all I'm doing is trying to get the customer to pick up the phone and call me, and giving them a relatively specific geographic area so that they know I service their locality. There are lots of articles on the web that explain how to optimize ad copy, maybe you should give them a read so you can be better than me, but I tend to keep mine pretty simple and to the point, and it seems to be working for me.

Whenever you set up adwords ads you also have the option of having them "mobile optimized" (better suited for cell phone viewing), "call only" (meaning when the viewer clicks on the ad they are viewing it from a cell phone and by clicking the ad it will call you instead of bringing them to your website), and other more advanced options Google has come up with.

I hope this is enough info to at least get you started with Google adwords. It is far from a complete guide, but it will at least steer you in the right direction while you follow the prompts to fill in the blanks. Yahoo Bing is almost identical in nature to Google Adwords; in fact, when I set up my Bing account I actually just imported one of my Adwords accounts. From what I read and experience however, Bing actually has slightly cheaper rates as far as the cost per a click, but that's due to less competition and less market share and reach on behalf of Bing as opposed to Adwords.

Beyond Google CPC, video advertising and banner ads:

Google also has platforms for doing video advertising (on YouTube as well as partner websites and apps/games) and banner advertising (on partner websites that sign up with them in return for sharing some of the ad revenue that come from displaying the ads).

With the video advertising, you can make a short (or long) video featuring your services and pay to have it displayed on Youtube.com (and/or Google affiliate web partners) when people type in certain search terms, or also based on their geographic location. If you make a good enough video you can get clicks and visits to your website for much cheaper than CPC, and at the very least you can get cheap views. I was getting my video viewed for between 7 and 10 cents a view. They only charge you for the view if the viewer watches the video for a predefined number of seconds or for a long enough percentage of the video time. You can also target the users interests (based on data Google collects), for instance to try to interact with individuals who have expressed an interest in moving, or buying a new home recently. I seemed to have a spike in web traffic to my site and call volume when I was doing video advertising, but I stopped doing it because I didn't have my callrail account and tracking set up at the time and couldn't tell for sure. I apologize for the lack of hard data I can provide on video advertising.

For banner ad image based advertising you can do either CPC (cost per click) or also CPM (cost per thousand impressions). These ads will show up on Google affiliates' websites, which get a cut of the ad revenue. I can tell you that without a doubt the major junk removal franchises and even some of your more local competitors are using banner ads and doing it profitably, so consider looking into it and setting up a campaign. This type of advertising is set up in a bidding type fashion like search CPC, with preference being given to those who are willing to pay more to have their ads shown. A realistic click through rate for banner advertising is much lower than search advertising. On average clickthrough rates for banner ads are around 0.1% or less, 1 out of 1000 impressions will get clicked in other words. If you do CPM on banner ads your cost per click on average might be lower than paid search ads, but maybe not by too much. See this link for more useful statistics and tips for banner ads: http://www.smartinsights.com/internet-advertising/internet-advertising-analytics/display-advertising-clickthrough-rates/

Facebook paid advertising:

One of the great things about Facebook paid advertising is that you can target not only peoples zip codes, but also their interests, and you can do it with graphics OR videos. I use facebook paid (and non-paid) advertising, and I'm telling you now that it works. Like with a lot of advertising though, you need to stick with it for at least a few consecutive weeks before you might start experiencing results. Not only can you pay for image/text and video ads, but if your ad pieces are savvy enough, they have the potential to be shared and posted between facebook friends and go a little if not a lot viral. This is great for exposure for your business, and also as a positive effect on your websites ranking on search engines if you have a lot of people searching for you for more info.

To do Facebook paid advertising, you will need to set up an account with a business page, and like with Google adwords, you will have to put a credit card on file with them to pay for your ads. The settings you select for your campaigns will be similar in nature to your adwords CPC campaigns, except with more options on targeting people's interests. The amount you pay for clicks and shares will also tend to be much cheaper than adwords CPC as well. I spend $200+ on facebook advertising a month to help keep a crew busy.

One little secret we have learned at my company is that when you are posting image ads, it's nice to have your workers in the picture loading junk/smiling even. You will get more exposure and shares if you make it more personal like this rather than just putting up pictures of your equipment and text saying what services you offer. We also like to take action shots, a few photos in chronological order showing us tearing down a shed or clearing a garage (before, midway, and after). You can also show your people at the scrap yard recycling the metal you get. The point is, get creative, and make it personal. You are trying to build a relationship with the facebook community with your ads, and if you want to build a relationship you need rapport, and rapport is personal.

Mini-Billboards

I've rented mini-billboards before and I can tell you from experience that they work well if you have a decent location. Mini-billboards, if you don't already know, are the smaller billboards (usually 4 to 10ft wide) that are lower on the side of the road and closer to the road or in strip centers, as differentiated from larger billboards which are usually very large (16ft and up wide) and by major highways. You can usually rent out a mini-billboard for $150-$200 a month per a side, whereas a major billboard may cost you $600-$3,000 a month, and you may have to pay six months up front. If you can get a mini-billboard near a major intersection or traffic stop, it should at least pay for itself. Look at it this way, if you can rent the billboard for $150 a month, and get $1,000-$1,500/month revenue from sales originating on this sign, then it fits within your relative 10% marketing budget. I've gotten one job worth $1,500 off a mini-billboard like this and then a few more the same month. Whenever you rent a small billboard like this, you will probably have to buy your sign separately, and have it designed/printed/installed by a local sign shop. This may cost you an additional $300 or so to get your sign up and running.

Another great thing about billboards is that you can reach audiences that aren't necessarily accessible through online advertising routes. This can include some of the older crowd who still have money, and lots of junk, but may not use the internet that much. You also get the advantage of that repetitive branding, and people that see your sign everyday on their daily commute will have your name memorized by the time the finally encounter a junk removal situation. I've even considered converting all my advertising to doing solely billboards.

Vinyl Lettering, Car Magnets, and Vehicle Wraps

I strongly recommend that at the very least you have car magnets on your trucks/trailers to advertise your business. They cost about $50-70 to have made, and they will definitely get you a few jobs and pay for themselves within a month or two. However, I prefer to take the advertising a step further and get my vehicles tatted up with large vinyl lettering. Vinyl lettering is basically like large stickers that sign shops can cut out and stick on your car with your business info. You see A/c repair vans, roofers, carpenters, and other contractors with them all the time, and that's because they work! You may pay close to $250-300 per a vehicle to get these custom printed and installed, but the business you get off them should pay for them within a year easy. For instance, three of my trailers are basically like 16ft long by 4ft high rolling billboards with my business name, phone number, and website on each side in vinyl lettering. I can go park them in busy parking lots or along busy roads and get a high volume of free advertising on slow days. If you have a box truck it can be an even bigger billboard.

If you want to take the vehicle advertising a step even further, you can have a vehicle wrap printed and installed by a local sign shop. I personally don't do this because the price is a little steep and I think vinyl lettering provides a good enough return on investment comparatively. Vehicle wrap design, printing, and install can cost $1,600 and up depending on your vehicle size.

Business cards and how to get the most out of them.

Getting business cards printed is kind of a no brainer. They are cheap for the value they provide and will get you repeat and referral customers. Depending on your supplier I think you can get something like a thousand printed for $40 or $50. No need to get fancy with the card stock and extra designs on the business cards for your junk removal business, leave the fancy upgrades for people like lawyers and architects where it might make a difference. Make sure you include all the relevant info on your card such as your phone number, email address, name, what you do/what you take, general service area, website, logo, and maybe even a picture of yourself to people can match a face to a name later.

Now, the important thing about business cards is what you do with them. Let me introduce you to the concept of the "six-pack" first of all. Any time you go out and do a job at a residence, you ought to be handing out five more business cards to the neighbors of that customer's house. Place your business cards in the crack of the door and resting on the door knob or door handle of the 2 houses adjacent to the customers house, and the 3 directly across the street from the customer, no need to knock. That way, you have 6 potential customers in the neighborhood, or a "six pack" (5 potential, and 1 repeat). It's a good way to target customers in affluent neighborhoods, and since you already got their neighbor they may have seen you and can ask the neighbor if you're service was worth it. Anytime you're driving through a neighborhood on the way to another job and you see a pile of junk in the front or side yard, you can also use this as an opportunity to put your business card on their door.

Anytime you go to a restaurant or grocery store, or other small business where they have a board or counter with business cards on it, you need to be putting your business card down as well too.

Another way to make use of your business cards is to map out all the local storage units in your area and go hit them up one by one to hand out your business cards, preferably on a slow day when you need to drum up more business. All you have to do is go in and ask if it's alright if you leave some of your business cards with them. Some will say no, so don't get bent out of shape when you get rejected, but many will say yes. Some will definitely want to hear more about how your service works so be prepared to give them a quick rundown. Some self-storage chains in particular will be more likely to say no, due to tighter corporate controls on what local advertising they will allow at the front desk, but the ones run by mom and pops are more likely to be much friendlier about taking your business cards and/or setting them on a display counter or pin-board. I've done this before and got a little surge in storage unit jobs afterward as a result.

You can also map out and go around to all your local realtors' offices and ask if you can give them your business cards. Many realtors will be excited to have a junk removal person in their pocket, and you will be surprised to find out how many people don't know what a junk removal business does, be prepared to explain. Realtors come across a lot of people who are moving (duh) so they are more likely to be able to refer your business than many other types of people. As a side note, realtors are sales people so it is basically their job to be friendly and network, so don't get too excited when they say they will definitely give you a call sometime. You will definitely get some calls from realtors, but don't overvalue their business and friendliness. While everybody and their mom seems to be a realtor or get their realtors license, only some are really into it.

Another place you can put your business cards to use is at Real Estate Investor (REI) Network events. People who flip homes or play landlord are likely to encounter the need for a junk removal business at some point if they do enough volume. Landlords evict messy tenants and home flippers buy trashy houses sometimes. As mentioned before though, just realize that these types of customers will expect slightly lower prices because they are business people and will shop around (or may already have their own maintenance crews), and because their jobs will often be larger and more frequent. This kind of networking is not for the timid though, while most are friendly, many of these people will blow you off in a hurry because you are, after all, trying to sell them something. To soften them up, you may mention that you do occasionally come across customers that are trying to sell their house because it is a wreck or has other expensive repair problems or situations, and that you could refer these customers to them, in return for a referral fee if they end up flipping or buying the house of course. This will actually be true, and is commonly referred to in the REI industry as "bird-dogging". In order to find these REI events, you can either join some of the real estate investing groups on facebook, or find REI event on meetup.com.

Thumbtack

While I have gotten some business from Thumbtack.com, I have found its usefulness for junk removal business to be limited. Thumbtack is a sort of paid advertising where potential customers post their specific job to the correct category on the Thumbtack website, and contractors are allowed to view the job and details, but not contact the customer and submit a bid for the job unless they buy and use thumbtack credits. Up to five contractors are allowed to submit bids for each junk removal job, and last time I checked you had to use 2 credits which cost $1.50 a piece ($3 total). The customer then selects the most favorable bid and contractor and contacts them directly to do the job.

I've gotten some customers from Thumbtack, but most the time I think I am either getting undercut by other local junk removal companies (but still paying to submit a bid), or just as likely the customer was not really serious/qualified in the first place. I also don't like the fact that I am competing for advertising space on the web with a company that is trying to get referral fees off me and play middle man. Furthermore, the job details submitted by the customer/thumbtack are often quite inadequate to submit a real, educated bid for the jobs. Finally, there is just not that much traffic on Thumbtack for junk removal jobs specifically, and most of the jobs that pop up are last minute weekend or end of the month move out events. I think Thumbtack is probably much more appropriate for other small business industries however, like lawn care for instance.

Yelp.com

Yelp is basically a small business review site, helping people to find local business within predefined categories. It is especially suited to the restaurant industry. I have gotten a reasonable amount of jobs from traffic from Yelp.com considering the very little effort I put into my businesses profile. As I have gained more positive yelp reviews, business from Yelp has gained more traction. I've looked into paid advertising on Yelp, but at first was told that they did not have enough "inventory" (search volume) to take on another junk removal advertiser. Months later I was contacted by a Yelp salesperson trying to sell me advertising, but I found that after reviewing the numbers of how much traffic they had and what it cost (like $800 a month to get started), it was not a good fit for my business and there are much cheaper advertising rates elsewhere. I just stick to the free profile they let me create.

Door Hangers

I've tried a short run of door hangers, and after reviewing my results and the literature available on response rates for door hangers, I'm skeptical about whether it's appropriate for a junk removal business. I tried a run of about 1,000 hangers, and paid $200 to have them printed. My wife and I distributed most of them in a very well-to-do neighborhood, as well as two other mediocre income neighborhoods. I got maybe 3 jobs directly from the hangers (a $250 job, a single item job, and another similarly small job), and maybe some name recognition later on down the line. Considering I spent $200 plus another 4 hours of labor at least (which I value at at least $50) to get $500 of revenue, I think this is not the way to go. Oh yeah, and I got one crazy lady who yelled at me for my door hanger and left me a bad review with the better business bureau and on Angieslist.com. Perhaps if you had a stack of door hangers handy in your truck in case you saw someone's house specifically that might need your services this form of advertising might be worth it, but I don't like the numbers on the untargeted route. On a side note, I have seen a College Hunks Haul Junk franchisee distribute door hangers to neighborhoods when they first came to my town and set up a new territory, but I think this was probably part of a grand opening campaign and I have not seen them do it continuously.

Bandit Signs

Bandit signs are called bandit signs for a reason; in many jurisdictions they are illegal and are considered an eyesore. I am in no way condoning the use of bandit signs with this book, but the idea does warrant some serious discussion. Bandit signs are those small 1 or 2 ft signs (usually hand written with a marker) you see staked into the ground off the side of the road (or taped or nailed to a tree, light post, or electric pole), typically near busy intersections, and more often on the weekends. Most often they will be advertising some residential service based business, like carpet cleaning, roof repair, carpentry work, etc, and another common thing they will advertise is "we buy houses".

Regardless of peoples' opinion on how trashy they look, or how illegal they are, I can tell you from experience that they do work, and they can get you calls. The calls you will get will often be lower quality customers than other forms of advertising, with some callers assuming that you haul off scrap metal for free for instance, but they can get you customers nonetheless. Chances are, your competition will be using bandit signs occasionally or frequently. I've even seen some of the big junk removal franchises use them. The upside of bandit signs is that they are a dirt cheap form of advertising. For about $1 dollar for the poster board, and 50 cents or a dollar for the stake to put it in the ground, you can get your phone number and message in front of literally thousands of people a day per sign at a busy intersection.

The downside of the bandit signs, however, is that they are illegal to varying degrees depending on the jurisdiction you place them. You can get fined pretty heavily by a city or county if you aren't careful and use some discretion in your approach. The subject of optimal bandit sign advertising is the subject of many informative free YouTube videos. More specifically, within the city limits of most cities is where you will receive the most recourse for bandit signs. The rules vary by city, but many have the right to fine you a few hundred dollars per a day, per an offense (per sign), and may take you to court sue you if you violate their rules and are caught. Many counties have similar rules, but from my understanding are a little more lax on their enforcement activity. Some jurisdictions will even call you out to a fake job or meeting specifically so they can fine you in person and prove that you were the one putting up the signs.

To avoid negative recourse, some people who put out bandit signs engage in some evasive maneuvers to avoid getting caught or fined. One common technique that I've heard about is to put a different number on the bandit signs than their usual business line. Usually a "burner" number, prepaid phone, or a Google voice number that Google lets people set up for free and reroute phone calls. Even with the Google voice number I've still read about bandit sign posters getting caught. Cities can still find your real name, or call you out to a fake job. The other most common tactic which seems to be more socially acceptable is to only put out bandit signs on the weekend, like early Friday or Saturday morning, AND THEN TAKE THEM DOWN at the end of Sunday or early Monday morning. Some jurisdictions even allow this schedule specifically, while others merely tolerate it because many of the municipal and county workers don't work weekends, so there is nobody on duty to catch the bandit sign placers. At any rate, be respectful of the local laws and consider the possible consequences if you plan on engaging in bandit sign activity, and don't say it's my fault if you get caught. I'm telling you NOT to do it.

Radio

Radio advertising is great for selling cars and furniture, but from the available literature I've looked up on successful junk removal advertising, radio is definitely NOT a recommended advertising channel. I don't know all the reasons or statistics behind it, but I've read that other junk removal companies have tried it but it wasn't worth it. I personally have not tried it. I definitely have never heard another junk removal company in the Houston area advertising on the radio. Be your own judge.

Angies List and Home Advisor

I used to love Angies List, until I tried some of their paid advertising, then I was quickly disappointed, stopped paying for the contract I signed, and had my entire business profile reset by them as a result, even though I had like 30+ positive reviews. Now I think I have 0 reviews. You, as a new junk removal business entrepreneur however, should definitely create your free Angies List business profile. You can and will get business from Angies List subscribers without paying for anything, and the more positive reviews you get the more traction you will attain, and thus more customers you will get. I just wouldn't recommend using their paid advertising.

I have heard other contractors swear up and down that Angies List paid advertising is legit, but these where contractors in fields where jobs sizes are typically much larger, like tree removal specialists and kitchen remodelers ($1,000-$3,000 and up revenue per a job), and where competence and skill are more important than price. In the junk removal industry however, workers don't need to be very skilled, and job sizes can be as low as $60 or $70, usually maxing out at $500 for a majority of jobs. People are more likely to just price shop.

Why is this a problem? I can give you personal examples of my problems with it. It can be a problem because on sites like Angies List, part of their paid advertising (at the time anyway) can include referring jobs to you for a fee, of like $20 or $30, whether you get the job or not. If you have someone price shopping for a single item removal, a fridge for instance, and they don't like your $75 minimum, they just move on and you pay a referral fee. If the job is a small job that is not a single item minimum fee job, like a $180 job, the advertising budget is still out of whack. For this reason, I also do not recommend signing up with HomeAdvisor.com, which offers a very similar service.

Another service that Angies list offered was a "Big Deal Coupon" where they email blast their member list with advertisement for your business and call it a discount (P.S. you don't really have to discount it), but they want 25% of the revenue of the first $100 you get from each job. The kicker is they collect the money from the customer, not you, and distribute it to you after they take their percent, and serve as a communication middle man when setting up the job, which lead, in my case, to a lot of miscommunication and unrealistic customer expectations as far as job size and price rates (you wouldn't know it by my positive reviews, but it was a hassle). I also paid to be put it their little magazine that gets mailed out every month too, and did not get a SINGLE job from being in that magazine. Overall I think I paid a percentage up front for an advertising contract and like $500 a month for a 3 or 4 months for Angies List referral jobs, advanced page placement, and ad magazine, and after I realized I really wasn't getting much return on my investment I quit paying the bill and told them I wanted out of the contract, which they definitely would not let me out of and wanted me to pay a large portion of the months remaining. The only paid advertising that you may organize to your advantage, potentially, would be the "big-deal coupon" if they still have it. I did get like 20 or 30 jobs in a month's time from the coupon thing, and some people pay for the coupon up front and then don't even use it.

Like with Angies List, I only recommend signing up for the free aspects of Home Advisor. I don't find the paid advertising aspects to be worth it.

SEO

Good SEO tactics are really beyond the scope of this book, but if you want your website to rank well on the search engines like Google, you will need to employ some good SEO strategies. SEO involves getting search engines to like you by increasing the amount of quality backlinks to you website, increasing the amount and usefulness of content on your site, increasing your website traffic, and increasing your social media presence, among other things. Some very basic things you can and should do include creating YouTube, twitter, facebook, pinterest, and LinkedIn accounts, and posting video and articles to them and interacting with them regularly. They should all have links to and reference your main website. In addition, you need to have a blog page or article section on your junk removal website, and you need to post articles to this page as often as you comfortably can because real content that people want to read is one of the major things search engines like Google are looking for. If you don't know what any of this means consider hiring an SEO specialist to do some of the work for you, but be wary of hiring SEO specialist without researching them first, as black-hat SEO and back-linking techniques can get your website de-indexed from Google or reduce your rank.

Setting up a service area and defining your market

Based on what I've read and experienced, I would say the junk removal market demographic is individuals 35-65 years old with disposable income, with a gender bias towards females who are less willing or unable to take on the physically demanding task of large item and bulk trash removal. I wouldn't really get much more specific than that as far as demographics, because I have all kinds of customers, it's just most of them are a little bit older, and female, with money. I think disposable income is really the most important part, it just happens to coincide with being older. The other aspect to this that I think is most noteworthy is that the best and biggest jobs usually involve a customer moving in or out of a home. This includes home buying and selling, evictions, deaths in a family or an inheritance, and also home repair and remodeling in preparation for or after a move. Usually there is some sort of event that spurs someone to NEED to get rid of the junk. Less frequently, you do get the customers that just decided it was time to clean up after themselves in a major way.

So, when setting up your service area, you definitely need to take into consideration how much DISPOSABLE INCOME people have, most importantly, but can also consider their age and gender. When you market to your area, you also need to consider, disposable income, as well as age, and other factors like whether people are interested in moving (maybe look at how old their home is), if you can. If you are tight on a marketing budget and you're doing some facebook ads, you might consider ONLY marketing to women, with disposable income, as a way of stretching your advertising dollar and getting more bang for your buck.

A FREE tool I recommend you use when defining your service area (unless you have access to some of the more advanced databases out there) is city-data.com's "income map, earnings map, and wages data" (see http://www.city-data.com/income/income-Houston-Texas.html for example). Below is a slightly zoomed in map of the city of Houston. The darker color areas indicate higher income, and the lighter color areas indicate lower income. Guess which areas I target? The darker color areas within about 15-20 miles of my headquarters, and I avoid the lighter color areas. So, I look up a zip code map and overlay income levels, and only target the higher income zip codes when I'm inputting my zip codes for Google paid search advertising and facebook advertising, it's pretty simple.

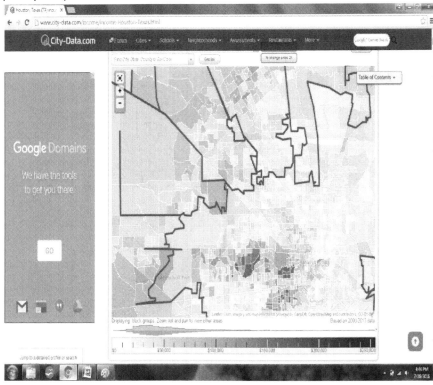

The other major consideration besides income levels you want to take into account when setting up your service area is whether you have enough people in your service area. Bare minimum I would say you need is 250,000 for your territory, but preferably more than that. It's no coincidence that this is the population size some major franchises junk removal companies will let you/make you purchase as a territory when you sign on with them.

You should also consider where the better cheaper landfills are in relation to your territory, as this will affect whether you can service a given area, or at what price you will be able to service it at if there are not favorable landfills or transfer stations nearby.

Chapter 5: Accounting, Payroll, Labor, Business Structure, and Tax Considerations:

Accounting and Payment Processing Software, and Payroll Too!

I'm going to keep this simple, unless you have an accountant to do it for you, just use intuit QuickBooks online. They charge by the month, with costs below $50 and depending on the depth of features you want. No I don't get a kickback for writing this. Make an online account. Then, link your business bank accounts that you made specifically for your business with the QuickBooks account. From then on your transactions will be imported into QuickBooks where you can categorize them, and also form reports like profit and loss statements, and balance sheets if you want. You can link your expense transactions and your income. It will make your Federal taxes a breeze too, because you can integrate their different accounting software products.

QuickBooks also has a credit card processing program, called "gopay", and you can get the smartphone credit card swiper gadget mailed to you for free. They make their money by charging 2-3% of credit card sales like most of the other credit card processers. You can link the gopay directly to your business account so that credit card sales will deposit directly to your bank account. I used to use PayPal when I started out for credit card processing, but switched to QuickBooks because it integrates better with all my bank accounts. You can get a bank to process credit cards for a cheaper percentage, but I want you to get set up right away without analyzing things too much. Progress not perfection!

You can also use QuickBooks as a payroll processesing software too, as an additional feature. It costs about the same when compared to other online payroll services, so why not use the one that is already linked to your bank account (costs about $30 a month to start, depends on number of employees)? The software will walk you through all the different federal and state dependent legal forms and steps you need to take to get set up to have an employee set up on payroll. You can also pay the federal (employees cut and employers cut) taxes on these wages through the QuickBooks account. Like I said, it makes it simple, about as simple as it can.

Business Organization, Employees, Taxes:

I suggest you organize your junk removal business as a Limited Liability Corporation (LLC). This should help protect your personal finances from liability your business may incur, including injured workers, damage to customers homes, and wrecks your big trucks and trailers are likely to get into eventually. A simple DBA does not protect you from these issues, it just allows you to open a separate bank account in your business name and collect state taxes in a business name. Forming an S-corp or other forms of corporations for a junk removal business, in my non-professional opinion, doesn't serve any advantage over an LLC and is more geared toward a larger enterprise, not someone just starting out. You should be able to form an LLC by filing it with your secretary of state. Sometimes government offices and websites are not very user friendly, so don't be surprised if you have to jump through some hoops and pay some fees. (Mine cost me $300 to form, and that's without a lawyer). All your business equipment and vehicles will need to be transferred to this LLC, and the insurance you buy will be under this LLC.

Make sure you get a FEIN (federal employer identification number) and use that instead of your social security number to open bank accounts associated with your junk removal business. This can be obtained relatively easily from the IRS website. You want to use this FEIN number instead of your SSN on any W-9s you fill out for contract labor (W-9 is what you fill out when you perform contract labor so your customer can 1099 you at the end of the year to report what they paid you and show their expenses to the IRS) so that shady contractors or companies can't try to steal your personal identity. You will also use this FEIN to hire employees.

If your state/county/municipality requires you to collect a sales and use tax, make sure you get the tax permit from your state comptroller office, and get it under your LLC. Make sure you keep a separate account for these taxes that you collect and pay on time. If there is a debate on whether you need to collect taxes for your junk removal service, make sure you talk directly with your local government offices to get the correct answer. When I started my junk removal business, many people were trying to tell me it was not a taxable service. If I had listened to them instead of doing my own due diligence I would either be in jail or paying back taxes right now.

When it comes to employees, my suggestion is that you only hire part time employees, not full-time, and start them off as contractors before you fully hire them. There are many reasons for this. If you hire someone full-time and business gets slow, you are responsible for giving them hours even if you don't have enough work, this means lost profits. Also, if they get lazy or complacent you've made your business somewhat vulnerable to their whims, and it will be much harder to replace them and retrain someone. It is also harder to operate your business when your full-time employee decides to call in sick or hurts their back, because you don't have multiple part time replacements. So, it is much better to have one or more part time helpers. This way, they are not completely reliant on you for full time employment, so if you have a slow day you can tell them to go to home early, or not come in at all. It creates flexibility to match when your customers actually need you. You can more easily fire a part timer with a bad attitude. They will also be hungrier for the hours you can offer them and may be more motivated. Junk removal can be very tough physically, so having part-time employees has an added benefit of giving them time to recover. It also makes it less stressful to downsize when you get to a slow season. As an example, look at the way restaurants do things. They have a bunch a part-time employees that work short hours (the restaurants rush hours) and are constantly on the hunt for more good hours. You will hopefully be a step above this restaurant type treatment of employees. To hire employees, I recommend starting them out as part-time contractors so you can test their work ethic before committing. This means having them fill out a W-9, and having them pay their own taxes for the first few weeks or months of working with you. Then it might be a good time to transition them to employee. This means having them fill out a W-4 and paying payroll taxes (state AND Federal) associated with having employees. I recommend using an intuit QuickBooks account to walk you through this process if you don't know what you're doing already. You can use is to calculate your payroll taxes AND pay them through the same app, as well as direct deposit to your employees bank account. Make sure you stay up to date on your payroll taxes. I pay them every time I do payroll.

Another consideration I have on getting employees is DON'T hire friends or family, or anybody else that you might have a problem firing or getting angry at or bossing around. You want to keep your business professional and profitable, and that often times means being a little cold hearted and getting people to do things they don't want to do, when they don't want to do it, and not putting up with any shit or excuses. Trust me, it is not hard to find employees. If you put up an ad on craigslist or facebook saying that you need unskilled part time labor help, and say what you're willing to pay, you can get 30-100 responses in a single day. There is no reason to put up with any crap from your employees; there are hundreds of people desperate for work that are willing to replace bad employees at the drop of the hat. The real due diligence you need to do is to pay for a criminal background check before you hire someone, and check their references. Another consideration is that their age and driving record will affect your insurance rates. If they are going to be a driver on your account, your insurance will be higher if they are under 30, or if they have had any "at fault" accidents in the past 3 years. So make sure you screen people for good driving records. Consider drug testing employees, because I can tell you from experience that a lot of meth heads have courted me for junk removal work in the past.

You should consider getting general business liability insurance for your junk removal business, especially if you are not partnered up with friends and family. This will cost you about $80 a month for a million dollar policy if you're still small, and should help protect you against damage to homes or businesses you're servicing. This does not protect you from any traffic accidents however. For your vehicles you will need to carry commercial vehicle "for hire" insurance, because you are transporting goods that people are paying you to transport. This will cost you at least about $150 per truck for liability insurance, and even more for full coverage. You will need to pay additional fees to insure any trailers you are towing (only like$10 or so more per month per a trailer). Not all companies provide this type of commercial vehicle insurance. For example, State Farm and GEICO could not provide my company with this insurance, so I had to go through Progressive insurance. As a side note, Progressive does not provide rental insurance, so if you want to rent out trailers/dumpsters on the side, you will have to find another insurance company.

Make sure when you're operating your junk removal business you do your accounting correctly to track all your business expenses because they will serve as a tax write of later when you do your federal taxes. This means you need to keep track of expenses for all the equipment and tools you buy, dump fees, supplies from home depot, labor expenses, office expenses, facilities expenses (if located in separate building from your home), phone bills, utility bills, advertising costs, gas expenses, repair expenses, bank charges, credit card processing charges, etc. This is pretty basic knowledge but there is one distinction when doing expense tracking that you will want to pay special attention to when running a junk removal business in particular. You want to separate out all vehicle repair/maintenance costs and gas costs from your other expenses. This is because when you do your federal taxes, you will have the option of claiming either vehicle repair/maintenance costs and gas costs, or claiming a mileage deduction at $0.55 per mile (at the time of this writing). You don't get to claim both as a deduction, you only get to pick one, so if you lump gas and repairs in with all your other expenses the accounting can get tricky to separate if you decide to go with the mileage deduction. And let me tell you, you're probably going to want to go with the mileage deduction because it usually ends up being larger. Consider having a separate credit card on hand for gas and repairs, that way the accounting becomes simple. In a similar vein YOU NEED TO TRACK YOUR

MILAGE on your vehicles to do your federal tax deductions properly. So, make sure you put a log in your trucks to track your vehicles' beginning and ending odometer reading. On a related note, vehicle payments if you are leasing a vehicle ARE tax deductable even if you are doing a mileage deduction, so there is a slight financial upside to leasing a vehicle rather than buying a new or used one outright. Unfortunately, this is offset by the full-coverage insurance requirements for a vehicle bought via loan.

Chapter 6: Junk Removal Business Cycles and Side-Businesses

Weekly business cycles, monthly, and seasonal concerns

Here is a very unfortunate piece of information for you; the junk removal business is largely a seasonal business. As a result, it can be a little difficult to scale up and open more territories because your expenses are not held constant compared to your expected sales, and your labor resources are hard to hold constant if you can't keep your workers busy. More specifically, your peak season will be spring and summer, but in winter and parts of fall, demand for your services will drop down to about 30% of what they are in spring and summer. This is based on my personal experience, as well as articles I've read discussing much more established junk removal businesses.

There are a few obvious reasons for this dip in business during the colder months, and probably many smaller circumstances that are harder to elucidate. First of all, a large portion of the good junk removal jobs originate from people moving or relocating. Home sales typically peak in spring and summer, and dip in fall, winter, and holidays. As a result, there is less demand for moving junk removal help during the colder months when people aren't buying as many homes and moving. Furthermore, when there is rainy weather there is less demand for junk removal help, because people don't want to move when it rains, people won't be doing projects outside when it rains (cleaning back yard for example), and rain definitely halts many different types of remodeling/construction projects, both residential and commercial. Additionally, customers are less likely to take on their cleaning project when it's super cold outside. I often compare people to bacteria. They become static and inactive when it's cold (like in a refrigerator), but when it gets warm they start to become active and permeate the world and reproduce. All these factors gets compounded I think by the fact that when demand for junk removal declines AND demand for construction/remodeling declines, the construction/remodeling type workers can become your competition because they are hungry for work and junk removal is not skilled labor. Basically anyone with a truck/trailer and marketing can be your competition. Holidays also will bring your junk removal calls to a halt, because people are doing family activities or traveling, and many will assume that you won't be open anyway.

I would like to reiterate that the weather will have a large effect on your call volume, regardless of season. If you have multiple sunny, nice weather days in a row, you will probably experience a much higher call volume because people are feeling good and going outside and tackling their projects, and moving and buying homes. But then when you encounter a few days of rainy dreary weather, the calls will slow down, only to pick back up again after a sunny day or two.

As far as weekly and monthly business cycles, pay special attention to the end of and the beginning of each month. People often close on their new homes at the beginning of the month, and tenants often get evicted or move out at the end of the month. So, you can expect larger, more ideal jobs around these times, and perhaps increased call volume as well. Also, many of these people will be on a strict deadline to get their stuff out of the house for the new owner or tenant, so they will be much more demanding as far as scheduling and deadlines to get their trash out. Unfortunately, everybody can need the same thing at the same time (like rush hour traffic), and this can put a strain on your resources to get everything done, so prioritize which jobs are better and more profitable and go after those with more intensity. When it comes to weekly cycles, I actually have a lot of my best days on Mondays and Thursdays. On Mondays I'm getting a lot of the left over junk from whatever project someone handled over the weekend. I'm not sure I can come up with a reason for Thursdays being good. I've looked at my website traffic before and it seems like there is more organic search traffic on Wednesdays so maybe that's why. On Saturdays and Sundays you get more demanding customers schedule wise because they need to get a project done on the weekend while they are not at work, and the landfills close early on Saturday and usually all day Sunday, so they wouldn't have a place to dump trash even if they knew where. Also, people move more often on the weekends and they have leftover trash. I used to think my phone should blow up on the weekends because of this, but really it's kind of random and hit or miss as far as call flow on the weekends. Maybe this is due to my advertising methods, or maybe demand is really just truly random. Overall, it's hard to pin down firm weekly cycles, but there are definitely monthly cycles, seasonal cycles, and weather cycles you should be able to anticipate.

So how do these seasonal cycles affect your business and what can you do about it? Well, there are a few different approaches you may consider. You may consider downsizing your staff during the colder months when weather cools down. This means you should hire part-time or seasonal workers during spring and summer and let them know that this may only be a temporary position unless you can stay busy. This is a common practice for lawn businesses, which may cut their staff in half when fall comes around. There are many people who won't have issues with this. You can hire college students and teachers for summer jobs for instance. Also, you need to plan your expenses more carefully and save more of the extra cash you get from the busy seasons. If you have big truck(s) you are planning on leasing, you need to anticipate having some slim months profit wise because you may not be able to keep all your expensive equipment busy. If you can barely keep 2 trucks busy during spring and summer for instance, you might struggle to keep 1 truck busy during winter, and that 2nd truck you have may just be sitting there burning money (lease/insurance expenses). You also may consider broadening your service area during slow seasons and taking on some jobs you would ordinarily pass on or refer out to someone else.

Another major option for dealing with seasonality issues is to have another side business you can fall back on and run alongside your main junk removal business, so that you can keep sales up and importantly, keep your good workers gainfully employed and happy. There are many service based side businesses that tie in well with junk removal and can be run concurrently or as a supplemental business during slow season. Some of them require more skill than others. For instance, a Christmas light installation business can be run during November and December, two of your slowest months. It doesn't require much education or capital to run, just some good marketing and some labor that does not fear heights. I have a friend in the tree removal business who uses Christmas light installs to keep his workers busy, because tree removal requests slow down during winter, and he can still go out and clear $500 profit in a day even though it's not his main gig. Another example is you might offer moving help during slow season. You may not enjoy doing moving help, but it can be profitable and YOU WILL get many requests for moving assistance, and may be the extra work you need to make it through winter profitably. I'm including a section in this book on side businesses you can supplement your junk removal business with.

Side businesses that complement your junk removal business

Moving:

This is at the top of this list for a reason. Because you will be helping so many people in the midst of a move, you will get many unsolicited requests for moving help, especially if you are nice to people and seem concerned with not running into walls or doorways when removing particularly large items. In fact, moving help is the other half of some major junk removal franchises' business plan; look up "College Hunks Haul Junk" for instance. You will need some moving blankets and extra dollies and a few other implements, but it is definitely within the realm of possibility. In some states you will need a license to do moving help professionally, and you definitely want to have some kind of liability insurance for movers if you do it on a regular basis. You don't necessarily need a moving truck, however. There are many moving helpers who just make the customer rent/pay for their own U-Haul and just charge an hourly rate, or you can rent a U-Haul or other moving company truck yourself. Typical charges for moving help might include $55/hr and up for 2 men. It's harder to quote flat rates for moving help so stay away from that unless you're more experienced, and make sure you have some kind of service minimum charge, like if you are charging $55/hr for 2 men have a 3 hour minimum of $165. I wouldn't recommend offering moving help for single items unless you have some kind of minimum charge, and moving help can get a little more complicated and in depth if someone is trying to move far away or out of state and they want you to truck it for them. Also, some large items warrant extra charges or another professional altogether, piano moving or safe moving for example. How to set up a moving service company properly is beyond my experience and the scope of this book. If you do offer moving help, you get the added benefit of getting larger junk removal jobs that extend from this.

Carpentry:

You will encounter many individuals doing remodel projects, or even investor types that need a whole house remodeled. If you have carpentry skills you are in a prime position to bid out and land some of these jobs. If you show up and do the trash job well, you've already proven yourself to be professional and developed rapport, and should have an easy time closing a sale.

Moving prep/packing:

When people are moving, they often have to spend a large amount of time packing up their belongings in preparation for the move. This is relatively unskilled labor that you can offer, and it puts you in a prime position to get a resulting junk job. Charge by the hour.

Professional organizers:

I occasionally get some junk jobs that are the trash left over from a professional organizer service that helped a customer reorganize their space. Some pro organizers are more skilled and advanced than others I'm sure, so you might want to do at least a little research on the topic before you jump into this. As an example, one organizer I've worked with a few times charges the customer $75/hr for two workers to come out help them organize/move around their junk, and the price also includes assembly of any shelving/cabinets/etc that the customer may need, but does not include the trash haul off. You, as a junk removal service, could offer not only professional organizing service at an hourly rate, but also trash haul as an additional charge.

Lawn business, scheduled repeat or one time:

You have trucks and trailers you can move lawn equipment with, unskilled labor to do lawn work with, people to answer the phone, insurance, etc. So if you get some mowers, blowers, weed eaters you have the infrastructure set up to lawn service on the side if you desire. This can provide a more steady income through repeat customers to offset the often intermittent workflow of junk removal. You can build up repeat clients, or perhaps you may just want to do one time, major lawn clean ups when the grass is over grown/trees need to be trimmed/brush needs to be cleared, etc for a high one time rate. My friend and I had a repeat customer lawn gig going along-side the junk removal when I first started, but unfortunately his trailer and several thousand dollars of commercial lawn equipment got stolen from in front of my house (lock up your trailers! Every time!) so we shut it down.

Pressure washing:

You can drop about a thousand dollars to get a relatively decent gas powered pressure washer, and then another $600 or so to get a rolling surface cleaner and extension wand/speed tips to get a pressure washing gig going on the side. Make sure you read up on how to not damage peoples siding and wood and how to use the soaps and detergents properly. You can make this money back pretty quick if you know how to market yourself effectively. If you can land some pressure washing gigs you can get paid $100 and up to pressure wash peoples driveways or decks, or get paid $250 and up to do a whole house depending on your area and house size and number of stories. Keep in mind that most of this is profit because you don't have any dump fees or extra trips to make to a landfill. If you can get 2 jobs a day at $250 each and pay a worker $120 in a day, you can clear $380 minus advertising and equipment expenses. There are some fine details on how to do pressure washing correctly, the correct equipment to purchase, and how to protect yourself from liability, but it's something worth considering.

Tree Removal/branch cutting:

Tree removal can be a business all by itself, but as a junk removal business you will actually get many unsolicited calls to remove trees for some reason. People will also call on you to cut down branches, or finishing chopping up and hauling off a tree that they already fell, or fell on its own. If you're interested in going this route, hopefully you already have some training for the serious tree removal jobs, but even if you don't do the serious more liability intensive jobs you may want to pick up some of the lighter branch cutting/tree removal jobs where you are not risking damage to someone's house. You can get a pole saw and chainsaw for relatively cheap and be able to make back your money pretty easily.

Demolition!:

As I mentioned earlier, you should strongly consider offering some kind of demolition services like deck removal, hot tub removal, shed removal, playground removal etc. For interior demolition gigs you can offer wall/sheet rock removal, tile removal, tub removal, sink removal, cabinet removal, paneling removal, door removal, carpet removal, laminate and other flooring removal, etc. Sometimes these jobs can be tricky to price out. It helps if you can decide first about how many man-hours it will take you, and then multiply that by what you consider your labor rate to be worth, and then add the waste disposal fee on top of that to come up with your final cost. I suggest charging $25-$35 per man hour.

Unloading Trucks/Random jobs:

You will get all kinds of calls and requests for random jobs, from unloading trucks to filling dumpsters to setting up tents. Make sure you have some kind of minimum charge in addition to a predetermined hourly rate to protect yourself from cheap people who want to nickel and dime you.

Dumpster/trailer rental:

I myself am venturing into the dumpster rental arena at the time I am writing this book. Dumpster rental and junk removal go hand in hand, and you will get many unsolicited requests for dumpster rental even if you don't advertise the service, so you might as well capitalize on it. If you can afford a roll-off dumpster truck and 30 or 40 containers it can be a whole other business. If you're like me though, you probably can't afford all that equipment when you are first starting out, but that doesn't mean you can't still make it part of your business. What I mean is that you can rent out extra trailers you have for people to use as dumpsters and operate it almost exactly like a roll-off dumpster rental business. For example, I have 3 dedicated 15-yard landscaping trailers that I rent out as "rubber wheeled trailer dumpsters". I make customers sign a rental contract when I drop the trailer off, and keep their credit card on file. You can secure the trailer with a ball lock and two wheel locks, and then put some wheel chalks in place to stabilize it. You set up a pallet and chain for a pull-off at the landfill, and make sure that your customers are aware of the prohibited materials and weight limit. The weight limit is the biggest difference (downside) as trailers typically shouldn't handle more than 5,000 pounds, so make sure your customer is acutely aware of this BEFORE you agree to rent the trailer. Once they fill it with their trash you go pick it up and dump it just like a regular roll-off container. You can upsell the fact that it is a rubber wheeled dumpster and is less likely to crack people's driveways. Make sure you charge extra for each day the customer holds onto a dumpster past the rental period agreement, $10-$30 per day extra for example.

Christmas lights:

As mentioned before, you can offer Christmas light installs during the slower winter season to offset a slower junk removal business.

Property maintenance and property management:

While operating your junk removal business you will encounter many opportunities to do lawn maintenance, painting, carpet cleaning or replacement, change locks, clean or replace toilets, etc. If you've got the skills and tools you can turn many of the contacts you make with property owners or investors into long term relationships that provide recurring revenue opportunities. Many property managers charge around 10% of gross rents to manage the maintenance of properties they control in addition to the cost of the repairs themselves.

Broker/sell leads:

If you can get into contact with some other junk removal businesses or dumpster rental businesses that are near, but outside (non-competing) of your service area, you may be able to work out a referral fee for sending them jobs that you don't want, or can't get to. I've done this before. It won't work out with businesses operators that aren't very professional, but some people will appreciate the value you can bring to them and will pay $5-$30 per converted lead, depending on job size. There are some businesses that take this idea to a whole new level by only advertising and setting up jobs for other companies without doing any of the actual work themselves. They are called brokers, and simply mark up the original vendors' service fee by whatever they need to make a profit. For instance I have a friend who works for a dumpster/portapotty/fence rental broker, and all they do is advertise a lot then mark up the prices of everyone else's services by 30% when they schedule the rental and take payment. I've been contacted by at least one national broker for junk removal jobs where they try to get bids by getting the customer to send pictures of the trash to be removed.

Valet trash:

You can offer valet trash services to apartment and condo complexes in your area as a way of creating an additional regular revenue stream to your junk removal business.

Deep clean properties:

Whenever a property is vacated by a tenant or just someone getting ready to sell it, they often need a "deep clean" before they put it on the market. All this means is they need someone to come in and scrub base boards/tubs/toilets/sinks, clean windows and blind, clean and vacuum carpet, dust, etc. You can charge $200-$300 and up to do a deep clean on a house depending on the exact details and if you have a qualified customer.

Junk Vehicle Removal:

I really wish I knew more about how to junk cars and boats profitably and legally. While I can't tell you how to do this, I can tell you that you will get a TON of calls from people thinking you are a junk car removal and/or parts junkyard. If you know anything about how to do this, you will probably be able to make some money off it. I guess some of the biggest concerns are how to dispose of all the fluids from the junk vehicles properly, and car title issues and legalities. I've gotten some car parts out of peoples garages off jobs and resold them just on craigslist, so I KNOW there is some money in this business beyond just the scrap metal value of junk vehicles.

Referring Distressed Home Seller Leads:

About a year into operating my junk removal business, I got a call from a local real estate investor asking if I ever encountered customers who had beat up houses or were really just needing to sell their home that needed work. He told me that his company was willing to pay $1,000 for such leads that they could actually close on, and all he needed was a phone number, address, the person's name, and a willingness to sell without involving a realtor. I talked to him on the phone for a minute, not thinking much of it, but when the right situation occurred a few months later (a customer flat out asked me if I knew anyone who wanted to buy a house), I passed along the info to my investor friend and boom, they ended up buying the house and I got a $1,000 check. A few months later a similar situation occurred and my investor friends wrote me a $1,500 check (they increased their referral reward). Needless to say, I got pretty excited at the prospect of just turning over someone's information and then getting a fat check in the mail. I started asking just about every customer if they were trying to sell their home. The next 10 or 15 distressed home seller leads I turned over to my investor friends yielded no results however, but I'm not saying that to discourage you, just to give you realistic expectations. The distressed home seller lead thing is a numbers game, and more like 1 in 30 of these leads is likely to close, I just got very lucky in the beginning.

The correct real estate investing term this situation refers to is "bird dogging". Investors frequently use "bird dogs" to feed them leads to potential opportunities that they otherwise would not encounter, and then reward them if they close the deal, but not if they don't. The people willing to buy these leads frequently refer to themselves as wholesalers, flippers, landlords, and real estate investors. Not all investors are equal, and some will only be willing to pay like $500 for a closed lead. Don't settle for something small like this, you should be able to get at least $1,000. Just look up real estate investors in your local area and shop around. Many will even have their bird-dog program detailed on their website. Consider going to a real estate investment networking event in your area and tell people there that you do junk removal and get leads occasionally. You will find that you have them very interested in you, and you may even get some trash removal work out of some of them, as they are in the home flipping business.

Chapter 7: Dealing with Difficult Situations

Evasive maneuvers: the art of dodging unrealistic people and situations

Inevitably you are going to encounter some very difficult people and situations while operating this business, or any other business for that matter. For that reason, it's important to have some predefined strategies for getting out of these situations if they don't deserve your effort. Think of it as basic self defense techniques against non-physical attacks. You can use these techniques in everyday life as well. Sometimes it's better to let customers down easy and tell a white lie rather than be totally honest and direct, which can create a lot of friction. I think it's always important to give yourself a choice. You don't HAVE TO do anything, that's for people who aren't self employed.

1. **The time crunch**

    Let's say someone calls you with a job you don't really feel like doing and you're not too desperate for cash, so you want to turn down the job without developing a bad rep as being a lazy business owner. Or maybe the person on the other end of the call sounds like a complete moron and you're afraid you won't get paid, or maybe they sound really cheap and just want a free in person quote first and you're pretty sure it will just end up being a waste of your time.

    One approach is to act like you're booked; you're running such a great business that you're too busy to do the job. So, if the customer is in a big hurry, tell them you can't get to it till a week from now. Or maybe they can only do it at 3pm on a Friday, tell them you already have a job scheduled for 2:30 and there is no way you can make it.

    What if you're already on a job and you've already filled your trailer to capacity and you're fed up with a customer for whatever reason, but they want you to come back to the same job and grab some more stuff that they didn't tell you about when they first scheduled. You always have the option of telling you can come back, but not today or this week because you've already booked a bunch of other jobs, or maybe you're about to go on vacation. Maybe your worker has to be home by a certain time because they have to pick up their kid. You get the idea.

2. Appeal to third party

There are many ways to appeal to a third party to avoid a situation or confrontation. I've considered many times of not letting anybody know that I own my own business just so I can avoid sticky situations related to being the main decision maker.

So let's say you have a customer that wants you to come down on price and wants to haggle, sometimes AFTER the job is done even though you agreed to a rate BEFORE starting the job (this happens occasionally). Tell them that your boss would kill you/fire you if you came back with that much money, and you have to stick to the written rates you agreed on, or else you have to unload the trailer. What if the customer wants you to move an armoire downstairs, but not haul it off for junk, but it is solid wood and 350 pounds. Tell them your boss doesn't let you do moving help, or it's against company policy because of damage and liability issues. What if you don't want to schedule a particular job today, tell them that your employee/co-worker called in sick today so you are shut down.

3. Out of area

What if somebody got you to agree to a job at a particular price at a particular time, but then throws in one extra curveball that totally changes the dynamics of the job, like it's in an unsafe part of the ghetto or in a high-rise condo, or the stuff is covered in rat poop, or there are also 3 yards of shingles in the backyard. You can always tell them that they're out of your area, especially if your area is not clearly defined on your website. Sometimes even if they told you their address already, you can tell them that you went and looked it up on the map because you weren't quite sure where it was, and sure enough, it's just outside your area. If you get really desperate you can even tell them that your company recently changed locations, and they used to be in your area, but aren't any longer. This is a good excuse if you have someone else taking calls for you and scheduling, and due to their inexperience they book a terrible sounding job. You can always call back and say out of area.

4. **We can do that, but…..**

You can always add extra conditions to your service that no one will agree to, or extra conditions that actually would make the job worth doing, for you personally or financially. For instance, if a hoarder house has a flea or tic problem, or a beehive in a wall (both have happened to me), tell them you can do the job, but they have to get an exterminator to get some kind of handle on the pest situation. Maybe the customer has a lot of loose trash everywhere in an overgrown yard that you would have to spend a lot of extra time picking up and hand excavating and they don't seem like the type that would be willing to pay you extra for the extra service this requires. Tell them that you require the trash to be bagged up if it is small trash like this. What if there is a bunch of tile or crumbly sheet rock in the back yard, and the back yard is large and sloping and is a 30 yard walk from where you can park? Tell them you require all construction waste to be either in the garage, or driveway, or be bagged up so you can carry it. You can also negotiate extra hourly rates if you don't think your junk hauling prices should include certain types of labor, and you can give overinflated labor rates if you actually don't want to take on that certain activity.

5. **Hand carry fee**

Some companies, not only junk removal but also businesses that do fence rental and install, will charge a "hand carry fee" if they can't park within a predefined distance of the job. For instance, you might add a hand carry fee for back yard construction waste jobs or upstairs trash jobs. $1 per extra foot travelled or $50 for a flight of stairs for instance.

6. **The I don't want to do this price**

I've used this approach to many excessively difficult/problematic jobs that are super gross and downright hazardous. If I don't really want to do a job, sometimes I will throw out a quote that is twice as high as I might normally charge. If the customer goes for it, it's partway worth it and you can always bring on extra labor or subcontract the job to ease the pain. Most times though, people will keep price shopping and you can move on and not punish yourself in the name of irking out a living.

7. **Refer to outside contractor**

This is by far my favorite because you can turn someone down but at the same time still help them and not lie to them. I have phone numbers of all my competitors (especially local non-national franchise ones) so I can steer jobs their way if I don't want to take them. I also have numbers for tree removal businesses, landscapers, handymen, people with excavators, cleaning ladies, estate sale companies, etc so that I can direct people to more appropriate service providers rather than trying to make junk removal service a kind of catch all for any kind of random job a caller comes up with.

8. **Equipment problems**

You can always say that your truck broke down, or one of your trucks broke down, or you had a flat on your truck, or trailer, so you won't be able to make a job, or make it on time.

9. Employee problems or your own physical health problems

Sometimes this will be dishonest; unfortunately it will also be true sometimes. You can tell people that your worker(s) called in sick or that you yourself are sick or your back is out from lifting something heavy

10. Dangers on the job, liability games

I've been on jobs before where it became apparent that the customer lied to me about one thing or another to get a better price. For instance, I did one rather large job one summer where I agreed to throw in the scrap metal for free, in large part because the guy had told me I would be taking a large amount of copper and also about 800 pounds of lead. Later after the job was mostly done he decided that I couldn't take the copper, and I found out that the lead was actually not lead. Instead he directed us to a bunch of broken window frames and other metals leaning against a fence that were intertwined with about 10 years of overgrown vines and trees saying he wanted that gone. I soon discovered there were a few bees and wasps in the vicinity, and this became my exit for the job. I told him my worker was allergic and that we would have to leave, and we could follow up later, but for now we had spent too much time there anyway and had to move on to the next job to stay on schedule.

The point is, if you encounter bees, wasps, poisoness snakes, scorpions, asps, centipedes, dangerous varieties of spiders, etc, this can be your exit point for a job gone south. Let people know that you don't have health insurance, or you don't have insurance to cover your deathly allergic worker. I've encountered all manner of scary insects and reptiles on the job, sometimes in places you can't see easily, and sometimes in situations where I would point it out to the customer but it's gone before they see it. Even if it's not there, you can still say there was a black widow or brown recluse and that it's no longer safe for you to continue the job. It's kind of hard for a customer to argue with that.

You can also claim that a structure is too unstable and unsafe for you to clear out, and in the right circumstances you won't be lying.

11. Weather concerns

Maybe you would like to not schedule a particular job, or control the schedule more intensely without appearing overbearing. You can sometimes blame it on the weather, saying that there is a high percent chance of rain on a particular date and time, or maybe its summer and its simply too hot to do an outside job at noon, so you need to schedule it early morning or later afternoon. You can use this sometimes to control the schedule without losing the job to someone else, because it's not unreasonable to think other contractors may say the same thing.

12. Order minimum that is excessively high

I'm pretty sure I've been to some junk removal jobs that another contractor either blew off on purpose or lost to me because their service minimum was too high. For instance, I've heard of people quoting $200 to remove a single item like a fridge because that's their minimum, or $300 minimum to fill a trailer over phone, even though the amount of junk the customer had would clearly only fill about half the trailer. This may be a nice way to blow off small jobs when it's too far out of your way, they want to schedule something only after hours or during peak traffic times, or it's a ridiculously heavy item upstairs like large reclining couches, big screen TVs, treadmills that have to be disassembled before they can even fit through a doorway (but they don't want to pay for that) etc. Another situation you may encounter is that people want to schedule you for the weekend because they are moving, but a lot of the stuff they are trying to get rid of they plan on trying to give away to friends and family for free, leaving you with a tiny non-profitable job during a peak time when you get there.

13. We don't have the insurance for that, permits

Some businesses/HOAs/offices require vendors to have business liability insurance, and for some office building type situations, you might want to make sure you have it even if they don't require it. Telling people we don't carry liability insurance and that my boss won't let us do these types of jobs is my go to excuse for high rise condos, some apartment buildings, and definitely large multistory office buildings. It's not a big deal to move a couch out one door way, but it is a big deal to move an office of large desks out two doorways, down a glass elevator, out another hallway and doors that don't stay open, out to a far away parking spot, and then try to get back in the same building that requires key cards. And that's if it will even fit in the elevator. Try carrying a 12ft marble top executive meeting table down a rounded staircase because it won't fit, not fun. Keep this in excuse in your back pocket for when customers really try to get you to commit to a firm price BEFORE telling you it's in a multistory building.

14. Parking problems

I've escaped one job in particular where someone deceived me about the dimensions and type of fencing they wanted demoed, and it was even more awkward because they were subcontracting out the job that they were supposed to be doing for someone else. It was an apartment complex area that luckily had just received a lot of rain and simultaneously had a lot of the street blocked off for some construction and road repair. I could have parked in one spot but the customer wasn't there when we first arrived so I claimed there were cars and trucks in any reasonable spot and escaped. Funny thing is I still got calls from the same guy trying to get me to do other jobs later. I saved his number and quit answering his calls. The most deceptive customers are often contractors trying to get a better rate and subcontract out your labor to do their dirty work.

15. Weight concerns

I did a back yard construction waste job before where halfway through the job the customer started getting an attitude with me over how long it was taking, whether or not everything would fit in my trailer, and the fact that I said I couldn't take a huge stack of bricks and concrete she didn't tell me about, and to top it off she was "unable" to move her truck out of her driveway so we could load things easier. We had loaded up to that point nothing but large deck boards, many of which I had to cut just to fit in my 16ft trailer. I still needed to get paid though, so when the trailer was about ¾ way full I pointed out that it was squatting a little bit and said that we were at our maximum weight capacity, and that we could come back and do the rest the next day but I still needed to get paid for what we did take today. I could have loaded more, bent over and taken it, but instead I got paid and left an angry lady to her own designs.

16. Sorry it has to be bagged trash

I've made scenes of junk jobs where other junk removal companies used this copout. They hauled all the big furniture and other large items (easier, faster, more profitable) till they were full, then told the customer they couldn't come back to get the rest for another week because they were booked. I've also taken on jobs that other companies lost because they told the customer that their policy was that all the non-furniture/large trash had to be bagged for them to take it. If you do require customers to bag their trash it will make your life easier, but expect to lose out on work.

17. Yea sure we'll be back, or let me get back to you

Let's face it; dealing with some people is not worth any amount of money. If they are expecting a return trip to a job you can leave the return date open ended saying that you need to check the schedule or discuss with your boss, and then you have the option of not picking up the phone when they call or texting them back some other excuse like your truck is broke down and will be in the shop for a few days or maybe a week.

If you're not good at thinking on your feet and you're talking to a prospect on the phone, rather than giving them a firm answer to their inquiry, you can always tell them that you need to talk to your boss, or your workers in the field and then you will call them back.

Companies use this strategy on job applicants every day.

18. Family emergency

You can use this to back out of a job that you're not at yet, or even a job you're in the middle of that just took a turn for the worse. All you have to do is take your phone out of your pocket, say "oh shit", and then tell the customer you've got to go, because ….. insert excuse here. "My girlfriend just got in a wreck" for instance.

19. Landfill is backed up, no trailer space

Let's say you sleep in accidentally, or you overscheduled yourself, or decided to take a little "you time" and treat yourself to a nice lunch, or maybe you underestimated how long a previous job would take. Rather than making yourself look bad and explaining what really happened, you can always blame it on a backup at the landfill, especially when it's raining. This will happen for real sometimes too.

20. Can you help me load that?

If there is an extremely heavy item or other difficult loading situation that the customer springs on you last minute, or wants done after normal business hours, you can put the ball in their court by asking if they can help you load it or carry it because your helper will be off, or its too heavy for you to lift. Chances are they will lose interest pretty quick.

21. I'm going on vacation sorry

Everybody is entitled to a vacation right? Yours could just always happen to happen on days of jobs you have no interest in taking on or continuing.

22. Just be honest

Often times honesty is the best policy, but just don't expect it to be easy. When you are honest with people in difficult situations it can easily backfire. Other times it just extends a bad situation and if you're dealing with a dishonest person it just continues their game. On junk removal jobs in particular, if you try to establish some type of boundary with a customer they will often act like they don't understand, and keep pushing their agenda. Prime examples include customers trying to get you to stuff more junk on to a trailer that is clearly full already, customers trying to get you to schedule after hours or on weekends, not understanding why certain things cost extra, not understanding that you have a service area that you won't go out of even for extra money, not understanding that you won't take hazardous chemicals and keep trying to load it behind your back, not understanding the concept of weight limits, etc. Honesty, in some cases would mean getting a bad review or losing someone's repeat business.

23. Save phone numbers of annoying people and don't answer

If you encounter unsavory customers or leads, always make sure you save their phone number in your phone so that you don't accidentally pick up for them later.

24. Rush fees

If someone is in a super hurry and won't take no for an answer, you can always try to tack on a rush fee to dissuade them or make it worth your while.

Equipment Problems/Dealing with Mechanics/U-Haul Trucks:

If you're first starting off in junk removal hopefully you already have a truck that you can haul trailers with or have a box truck or a truck with a dump bed. Unfortunately, hauling all this trash around the city will start to wear on your truck, and you will quickly find yourself in need of repairs, repairs that need to be done in a hurry because you can't earn money without your trucks. So, you need to make sure you have some reputable mechanics in your area that you can work with. I'd like to recommend that you look up reviews on the mechanic shops local to you and ask for referrals from your friends for mechanics that they trust, but NOT mechanic shops that their friends own or work at. If it's a friend of a friend you can easily have issues with being able to really hold the mechanic accountable if their work or business ediquette is not up to snuff. Also, don't hire mobile mechanics off craigslist. I can tell you from experience that a majority of these people are amateurs that do terrible mechanic work on the side because they are too irresponsible or incompetent to own their own shop or work for one. I recommend finding established mechanic shops run by old men (not young) who are more likely to have a ton of mechanic wisdom and experience. Whenever you do drop a vehicle off, never tell them to take their time or that you're not in a hurry. Politely make it clear that you depend on this vehicle for work and try to get a clear date on when you can come get it by. Also, never drop more than one vehicle off at the same shop at once. If they start screwing up they have really got you by the balls if you are too dependent on their service. Often times good mechanics will be very busy (like they have a month's worth of cars to work on), so don't be hesitant to call around to see who has availability to take care of your truck quickly. Keep your options open, and you will often find that the first time a mechanic works on your vehicle they will be very ambitious in their efforts to make you happy, but after you come in a few times, the level of service may fall off and they may take you for granted.

So what do you do when your truck is in the shop getting worked on? What is the backup plan? If you have used trucks you're bound to have issues eventually, so you definitely need some sort of contingency plan. If you have friends or family that have large trucks you can borrow, that might be your first option. But after that, I recommend renting U-Haul. It's kind of crazy to me, but U-Haul offers many of their 1-ton trucks for rent at a cheaper rate than other car rental places rent out their small cars, and with less restrictions (lots of mileage not withstanding). For between $20-$40 a day plus mileage, you can rent a 10ft or larger box truck that can haul your trailers or trash. I don't know U-Haul's opinion on carrying trash in their trucks, but I can tell you I've done it. I don't recommend using their F150s or Chevy 1500s to haul trailers (the leaf springs are not thick enough to haul 7,000 pounds, regardless of what the specs say, you will fishtail), but their 1 tons (dually rear axle) are great.

I've looked into other temporary truck leasing/rental places, but U-Haul definitely stands out as the cheapest. Like I said, they typically charge about $30 a day, and then add a mileage fee of close to 0.69 per a mile last time I checked. So, after gas, you end up paying about a dollar a mile. This is nothing to scoff at, as it will add up quickly if you are busy doing about 100 miles a day, but it will at least keep you in business and on the road if you have one or more of your work trucks break down. This is NOT a viable option to use as your work truck permanently though, as the costs will quickly add up to be more than buying a new truck. Another thing to consider with U-Haul is that they often run out of inventory during peak moving times (weekends and the end of the month), so make sure you schedule as far ahead as you can to secure your rental when the need arises.

If you really wanted to try out this junk removal stuff and get your feet wet without too much upfront investment, you could even just run some ads on craigslist and facebook groups (free) and then rent a U-Haul on a Friday and/or Saturday to pick it all up and take it to the landfill. A lot of people are more than happy to schedule jobs on the weekends because they are off work, so you could probably stack up 2 or 3 jobs for the same day and make it a profitable run in a large box truck. Just make sure you know what hours your local landfills are open. So what if you have to pay a $130 rental fee if you do $800 in business and pay $100 in dump fees. That's potentially $570 for you and a buddy to split for one day's work, not to mention some cool stuff you might get to resell.

Chapter 8: Answering the Phone and Scheduling Jobs

Answering the Phone:

Make sure you are friendly and at least slightly energetic when you answer the phone. Don't just answer the phone by saying "hello" or "this is John". Identify yourself, your company, and ask how you can help. Here is a call example:

You: "Hi this is Mike with (company name) Junk Removal, how can I help you today"

Customer: Yes I was wondering about how you guys charge and how your service works

You: Sure I can tell you about that, but first real quick can you tell me what part of town you're on, just to make sure we service your area?

Customer: We are on the Northwest side

You: Ok great, we go there. So the way our service works is we send out 2 guys and a 16ft landscaping trailer, and you point to what you want gone and we load it. Our prices are based on volume. So, to fill our 16 ft long by 6.5 ft wide by 4 ft high trailer ALL the way we charge $400 plus tax, BUT, our services are prorated, so you only pay for the amount of trailer space you actually use. For instance, ¾ way full would be $300, ½ way full would be $200, ¼ way full would be $100, does that make sense?

Customer: Sure, I get it

You: Okay great, what kind of trash did you have?

Customer: Well we are moving out, so I have a few things I need to get rid of before we close on the house. We've got a couch inside the house, a few shelves and some other random junk in the garage, and then an old barbeque pit and some trash in the shed in the back yard.

You: Okay no problem, when were you hoping to have this gone?

Customer: Do you guys work Saturdays?

You: Yes we do work Saturdays, what time this Saturday would work for you?

Customer: Could you come around noon?

You: Yea sure no problem, would about 1pm work for you?

Customer: Yea that sounds good. Do you take credit cards?

You: Yes no problem. Could I go ahead and get your address?

Customer: Sure, it's 12345 Fake Address Ln, Blabla Houston TX.

You: Ok got it. So on Saturday what we'll do is shoot you a text to give you a thirty minute heads up when we're actually on the way, that way you know EXACTLY when to expect us, but it should be very close to 1pm. By the way, how did you hear about us?

Customer: Oh, I just did a Google search and you guys popped up.

You: Okay great, thanks for the info. We will see you Saturday then.

Customer: Sounds good. See you Saturday.

There are a few basic things I would like to point out about this call example. First of all, many customers have no idea about how a junk removal service works or how they charge. Get used to explaining how your service works, and how you charge, because you will get asked this over and over and over and over. Also, note that this person didn't raise any objections about the price, but didn't seem excited about it either. However, at least a third of the people who call will say, in one way or another, that they think your prices are too high. They may say it directly, or they may say it another way by telling you they will call back, or they have to check with their husband, or they are just calling around getting pricing, or in a lot of cases they might try to get an exact price over the phone by telling you in much more detail about exactly what they have so that they can nail you down to a price range so they don't fear a high pressure situation when you do arrive and possibly want more money than they are willing to spend. Get used to price objections; it's just a part of doing this business. It doesn't mean you should lower your prices, it means people don't always have realistic expectations about what your service should cost. For every one person that has a problem with your prices, there is another one that doesn't care and just needs their trash gone. Another thing to point out is that you will need to determine the customer's approximate location before getting into a long discussion about what they need. There will be A LOT of customers calling you from outside your service area, some of them by accident, and some of them that damn well know they are outside your service area but are in such a remote far out area that no one is willing to service their area so they call around trying to see if they can bend the rules a little bit. Note that I also asked the customer how they hear about my company. This is so I know what parts of my advertising are working. I also told the customer how they will know when I will be arriving. If you want to widen the time window you have to arrive at a customer's address, make sure you communicate over the phone that the customer should be at home waiting for a specified time window, and that times are not exact. As a general rule of thumb, there are 6 pieces of information you will need to get over the phone for every junk removal job:

1. What type of junk they have
2. Where the junk is at on their property
3. Their address (make sure you get zip code too)
4. When they need it gone
5. How they heard about you.
6. What's the BEST number to reach them at

Additionally, you will want to feel the customer out to make sure they have realistic expectations about your pricing so there is not an issue or confrontation once you start loading, or worse, after the work is done.

Scheduling Jobs:

As discussed previously, on a good day one crew might be doing 3 or 4 medium to large jobs. When you're on the phone scheduling new appointments, you need to be considering how far each job is from the next one or from the landfill and whether you will need to dump the contents before going to the next job, how much trailer space each job may take, how long a specific job may take to load, and other less obvious considerations such as rush hour traffic in the morning and afternoon, school zones, and lunch breaks your workers should be taking. All these considerations are likely to screw up your logistics if you don't leave enough time between jobs, or don't give your crew a large enough time window on when to arrive. I usually schedule most of my jobs 1.5 to 3 hours apart, which usually gives me enough time to do 3 or 4 jobs and not make my customers disappointed by making them wait excessively long. It also allows time to make it to the landfill between jobs when needed, or time to come back to my shop to combine or sort through loads between jobs. For single items like couches or refrigerators that happen to be on the same side of town and that can be combined into the same trailer, I might even schedule jobs 30 minutes apart, but for larger furniture/household waste jobs I might allot 2.5 hours for travel and load time, and for large construction waste jobs I might set aside 3.5 hours for travel and load time, because construction waste typically takes the longest to load. As a general rule though, schedule jobs 2 hours apart. Also, allow at least 30 minutes for landfill disposal time because sometimes the landfills will get backed up.

Conclusion:

With this book I sincerely hope I have helped you start your own junk removal business or at least found a way to make your existing business more profitable. Sorry if some of the language or editing was a little rough. I'm not really an author; I haul trash for a living. Thank you for taking the time to purchase this book and read it. Best of luck to you!

Thanks,

Mike

Printed in Great Britain
by Amazon